Understanding Rett S

Understanding Rett Syndrome offers a concise, evidence-based introduction to Rett Syndrome (RTT), covering a range of topics from diagnosis and causes to treatment and family management. It focuses on improving the quality of life for those with the syndrome by suggesting practical ways of managing the condition at home and at school, offering support and guidance to all parents and caregivers learning how to help children with RTT.

Over the course of six chapters, Fabio, Caprì, and Martino explore signs and symptoms of RTT, along with an overview of treatment, therapy, and interventions for those living with the condition, focusing on technological aids such as eye-tracking and ICT and new neural techniques.

Illustrated with interviews with parents of children living with RTT, *Understanding Rett Syndrome* is essential reading for parents and caregivers, as well as practitioners in clinical and educational psychology, counseling, mental health, nursing, child welfare, public healthcare, and those in education.

Rosa Angela Fabio is Full Professor of General Psychology at the University of Messina, Italy.

Tindara Caprì is Contract Professor at the University of Messina, Italy.

Gabriella Martino is a Researcher in Clinical Psychology at the University of Messina, Italy.

Understanding Atypical Development

Series editor: Alessandro Antonietti
Università Cattolica del Sacro Cuore, Italy

This volume is one of a rapidly developing series in *Understanding Atypical Development*, published by Routledge. This book series is a set of basic, concise guides on various developmental disorders or issues of atypical development. The books are aimed at parents, but also professionals in health, education, social care, and related fields, and are focused on providing insights into the aspects of the condition that can be troubling to children, and what can be done about it. Each volume is grounded in scientific theory, but with an accessible writing style, making them ideal for a wide variety of audiences.

Each volume in the series is published in hardback, paperback, and eBook formats. More information about the series is available on the official website at: https://www.routledge.com/Understanding-Atypical-Development/book-series/UATYPDEV, including details of all the titles published to date.

Published Titles

Understanding Tourette Syndrome
By *Carlotta Zanaboni Dina and Mauro Porta*

Understanding Rett Syndrome
By *Rosa Angela Fabio, Tindara Caprì, and Gabriella Martino*

Understanding Rett Syndrome

A guide to symptoms, management and treatment

Rosa Angela Fabio, Tindara Caprì, and Gabriella Martino

Routledge
Taylor & Francis Group

LONDON AND NEW YORK

First published 2020
by Routledge
2 Park Square, Milton Park, Abingdon, Oxon OX14 4RN

and by Routledge
52 Vanderbilt Avenue, New York, NY 10017

Routledge is an imprint of the Taylor & Francis Group, an informa business

British Library Cataloguing-in-Publication Data
A catalogue record for this book is available from the British Library

Library of Congress Cataloging-in-Publication Data
A catalog record has been requested for this book

ISBN: 978-1-138-60055-3 (hbk)
ISBN: 978-1-138-60056-0 (pbk)
ISBN: 978-0-429-47085-1 (ebk)

Typeset in Sabon
by Deanta Global Publishing Services, Chennai, India

Contents

Chapter 1

Signs and symptoms of Rett Syndrome

The earliest descriptions of the syndrome, dating back to 1954, were given by Andreas Rett, an Austrian pediatrician, the syndrome later being named after him. It is a rare pathologic condition, almost exclusively typical to the female gender, normally characterized by altered mental and psycho-behavioral development, with symptoms showing a few months after birth in apparently normal conditions. The first part of the chapter deals with the evolvement of the syndrome, which is quite rapid, reaching maximum severity in most cases. We will also argue the clinical features of the full-blown condition. These features can be promptly identified with specific, stereotyped behaviors, such as waving and rubbing of hands, beating of the chest, biting fingers, sudden shouting, a lack of interest in the immediate surroundings, microcephalism, severe intellectual disability, and hypotonia. In the second part of the chapter, comorbidities will be dealt with: epilepsy, delayed growth, dysautonomia, adverse bone health and scoliosis, and sleep disturbances.

1.1 Features of Rett Syndrome

In 1966, Andreas Rett reported for the first time the clinical features of the syndrome that would later bear his name. His work consisted of a description of young females with similar characteristics and represented a milestone of this field (Rett, 1966). Rett was initially impressed by almost identical stereotypic hand movements, which represented the first description of the gestalt of Rett Syndrome (RTT) whose clinical diagnosis has been progressively refined to the last publication of revised diagnostic criteria in 2010 (Neul, 2010).

RTT as a new nosographic entity was introduced by Bengt Hagberg and colleagues who identified clinical signs in their own patients, and their publication represented the initial clinical description of 35 cases of RTT in the literature in the English language (Hagberg et al., 1983).

Since Rett's first recognition of it in 1966, several papers on RTT have been published, and the identification of genetic causes of this syndrome represented a boost to the research on this topic.

The classic signs and symptoms of RTT include many functional impairments, leading to the substantial necessity for support in daily life, rendering the patients a social and economic burden, and requiring parents and caregivers to also be deeply emotionally involved. The classic clinical features of RTT consist of severe functional impairments, which are characterized by either gradual or sudden loss of hand and communication skills, loss of balance, and development of hand stereotypies (Lee et al., 2013; Leonard & Bower, 1998; Neul, 2010). Significant associations between pattern genotype and the clinical hand and gross motor skills exist (Bebbington et al., 2008; Downs et al., 2010, 2016a; Fehr et al., 2013).

At the onset of the clinical manifestations, subtle changes in development often precede the regression, which is characterized by either gradual or sudden loss of hand and communication skills, balance and presence of stereotypies (Fabio et al., 2009). The first signs often include reduced hand control and a decreasing ability to crawl or walk normally. Eventually, muscles become weak or may become rigid or spastic with abnormal movement and positioning (Lee et al., 2013; Leonard & Bower, 1998; Neul, 2010).

Parents often say that the symptoms usually noticed first are floppy hands and legs, incessant crying, and the obvious disappearance of previously acquired skills. They also observed that if their child had been able to speak a few words or walk several steps before the onset of the symptoms, she would gradually lose the skills she had gained and in time, she may lose the ability to speak and walk completely. She will develop stereotypical behavior such as wringing, clapping, or patting of hands. However, the progression of RTT varies from one child to another. For example, some parents note that their daughter has lost her ability to walk, others that she is still able to, but will display a stiff-legged walk. Lucia, the mother of Teresa says:

> "Our daughter Teresa was almost two years old when she began struggling to walk, to crawl and to talk ... she repeatedly clapped her hands".

Originally, RTT was recognized solely on the basis of a clinical diagnosis, considering the Vienna diagnostic criteria and later, recommendations by American researchers. For epidemiological research, it was recommended to include only patients diagnosed as classic cases of RTT. Later in time, subjects not fulfilling all the necessary criteria were also considered as atypical RTT, such as congenital, childhood seizure onset, male, late childhood regression, and preserved speech variants (Goutières & Aicardi, 1986; Trevathan, 1989; Zappella, 1992). For example, Hagberg and Skjeldal (1994) suspected atypical RTT development in a ten-year-old girl with intellectual disabilities and he thought that the diagnosis required the presence of three or more primary criteria and five or more supportive criteria.

Today, clinical diagnosis involves a slight expansion of the exclusion criteria, and the evaluation of new criteria relating to breathing dysfunction, peripheral vasomotor disturbances, seizures, scoliosis, growth retardation, and small feet (Hagberg et al., 1985; Neul, 2010).

In accordance with the revised diagnostic criteria and nomenclature by Neul (2010), the clinical picture associated with typical RTT is defined by a regression of purposeful hand use and spoken language, with the development of gait abnormalities and hand stereotypies. After the regression phase, a period of stabilization and potentially even improvement follows, with some patients partially regaining skills. This potential for some skill recovery emphasizes the importance of the acquisition of a careful anamnesis to determine the presence of regression (Neul, 2010).

As there are no clear signs of impairment until the age of six months, parents and primary clinicians are usually not concerned about development which seems to be in line with a physiological one.

In the atypical RTT, known as the congenital variant, there is early abnormal development from birth; that is the reason these forms should be evaluated using the atypical RTT criteria.

In recognizing RTT, clinicians and teachers sometimes detect some suggestive clinical features and refer children for comprehensive evaluation due to the presence of signs or symptoms such as slowing in the rate of head growth, breathing abnormalities, and the intensive "Rett gaze" used for communication. These clinical manifestations are reported in the criteria for atypical RTT too (see Table 1.1).

It is known that RTT may also be observed in males, although initially it was recognized only in females, and that specific genotypes may be associated with different signs and symptoms, and may also be associated with severe cases of the syndrome (Bebbington et al., 2008; Downs et al., 2010, 2016b).

Adults with RTT but who have preserved the capacity to walk have a mutation associated with a milder phenotype (Anderson et al., 2014;

Table 1.1 RTT diagnostic criteria

RTT diagnostic criteria 2010	
Required for typical or classic RTT	*Exclusion criteria for typical RTT*
1. A period of regression followed by recovery or stabilization 2. All main criteria and all exclusion criteria 3. Supportive criteria are not required, although often present in typical RTT	1. Brain injury secondary to trauma (peri- or postnatally), neurometabolic disease, or severe infection that causes neurological problems 2. Grossly abnormal psychomotor development in first six months of life
Required for atypical or variant RTT	
1. A period of regression followed by recovery or stabilization 2. At least two of the four main criteria 3. Five out of eleven supportive criteria	*Supportive criteria for atypical RTT* 1. Breathing disturbances when awake 2. Bruxism when awake 3. Impaired sleep pattern 4. Abnormal muscle tone 5. Peripheral vasomotor disturbances 6. Scoliosis/kyphosis
Main criteria*	7. Growth retardation
1. Partial or complete loss of acquired purposeful hand skills 2. Partial or complete loss of acquired spoken language 3. Gait abnormalities: Impaired (dyspraxic) or absence of ability 4. Stereotypic hand movements such as handwringing/squeezing, clapping/tapping, mouthing, and washing/rubbing automatisms	8. Small cold hands and feet 9. Inappropriate laughing/screaming spells 10. Diminished response to pain 11. Intense eye communication – "eye pointing"

* Consider diagnosis when postnatal deceleration of head growth observed.

Foley et al., 2011). In the same way, for communication skills, those with milder mutations such as Arg133Cys or Arg306Cys are more likely to learn to babble or use words before regression, to regress later, to retain some oral communication skills and the capacity to walk after the regression phase, and to be diagnosed later (Anderson et al., 2014; Fehr et al., 2011; Foley et al., 2011; Urbanowicz et al., 2015).

1.2 RTT and comorbidity

The RTT phenotype may include several manifestations of associated comorbidity. In this section, we describe the most common forms of comorbidity.

1.2.1 Epilepsy

Epilepsy is very frequent in patients with RTT, occurring in about 80% of subjects; seizures are often difficult to treat, and in several patients, anti-epileptic drug polytherapy is needed (Bao et al., 2013; Glaze et al., 1987, 1998, 2010; Jian et al., 2006, 2007a; Nissenkorn et al., 2015; Steffenburg et al., 2001). It is well known that refractory epileptic seizures can be associated with neuropsychological impairment involving different cognitive functions, such as memory, attention, and mental speed (Aldenkamp & Bodde, 2005). In this field, the study of Vignoli and colleagues (2010) was aimed at delineating if, and how, neurological and neurophysiological impairment reflects behavioral and neuropsychological functions, and identifying prognostic factors that could be important in the clinical management of girls with RTT. In particular, the main purpose of this study was to verify if neurophysiological and epileptological characteristics could be correlated with cognitive measures, obtained using eye tracker technology, and behavioral scores (Vineland Adaptive Behavior Scales and Rett Assessment Rating Scale) in 18 patients with RTT (mean age 13.7 years) at clinical stages III and IV. Age at epilepsy onset and seizure frequency were strictly correlated with neuropsychological outcome, as were electroencephalogram (EEG) stage and distribution of paroxysmal abnormalities. The results of the study of Vignoli and colleagues (2014) demonstrated that neurophysiological features should be considered prognostic of cognitive and behavioral outcome in the clinical management of RTT. Moreover, these findings indicated that both epilepsy features (age at seizure onset and seizure frequency) and EEG characteristics (EEG stage and EEG abnormality pattern) are correlated with the ability to recognize and match pairs and semantically categorize with respect to animals and behavioral features, as assessed with the Vineland Scales and Refractory anemia with ringed sideroblasts (RARS). The significant ability to recognize and categorize animals, but not the other objects proposed in the task, may be explained by these girls' greater knowledge of animals as compared with fruits and emotions.

Regarding the relationship between age at epilepsy onset and cognitive impairment, the study of Vignoli and colleagues (2010) showed that in girls with RTT, epilepsy also plays a crucial role in future cognitive performance, as demonstrated by recent studies supporting the assumption that the epileptic process underlying seizures could interfere with cognitive development (Kaaden & Helmstaedter, 2009). In addition, in the group of patients with RTT, age at seizure onset was inversely correlated with the ability to recognize emotions, as it has been exhaustively shown in patients with temporal lobe epilepsy involving the temporomedial structures and especially the amygdala in whom early onset of seizures/epilepsy is a key factor leading to severe impairment in the recognition of emotions (Meletti et al., 2009). This is also supported by the recent finding in a mouse model in which specific deletion of MeCP2 in the basolateral amygdala mediated behavioral phenotypes associated with RTT, impacting selective forms of learning and memory (Adachi et al., 2009).

With respect to seizure frequency, factors influencing the course of epilepsy in RTT are not yet well understood. It has been shown that compared with later onset, early epilepsy onset tends to be associated with more severe epilepsy, including more seizure types, more frequent intractable epilepsy, and status epilepticus (Steffenburg et al., 2001). Moreover, children with RTT with early developmental problems as well as those with greater motor disability have a higher seizure frequency (Jian et al., 2007a).

Looking at EEG features, we found that as soon as EEG abnormalities became more diffuse and multifocal, cognitive performance decreased. This finding could be explained by presuming that epileptiform EEG discharges could have additional effects on cognitive processes (alertness, mental speed) that might accumulate over time, resulting in stable effects (Aldenkamp & Arends, 2004).

With reference to diagnosis of epilepsy, even if the EEG is diffusely abnormal, typically from about 18 months of age, this finding does not necessarily reflect seizure activity, and many events characterized by caregivers as seizures are not associated with abnormal EEG findings; thus epilepsy diagnosis is still difficult to reach (Glaze et al., 1987, 1998). In the cohort studies, epilepsy was diagnosed in up to 95%, with a median age of onset of 4 years, although seizure frequency declined with age and was lower in subjects with Arg294X or Arg255X mutations and higher in subjects with Thr158Met mutation (Bao et al., 2013; Glaze et al., 1987, 1998, 2010; Jian et al., 2006; 2007; Nissenkorn et al., 2015; Steffenburg et al., 2001).

1.2.2 Growth deceleration

Another manifestation of comorbidity is the growth retardation that was reported among the supportive criteria for RTT. Head growth deceleration occurs first, followed later by slowing of weight and height increase, with a definite relationship with genotype (e.g. Thr158Met, Arg168X, Arg255X, Arg270X) (Tarquinio et al., 2012). Vasomotor signs at the extremity (e.g. cold and blue hands and feet) may represent additional clinical findings for RTT, although the prevalence is poorly investigated and the genotype association is not known yet (Julu et al., 2001).

Beyond neurological impairment, the abnormal motor skills are thought to promote the higher incidence of scoliosis as a common skeletal deformity encountered in up to 75% of girls by the age of 15 years, especially in those subjects with the most severe mutations (e.g. Arg255X) or the large deletions (Downs et al., 2016b; Percy et al., 2010). Scoliosis is usually progressive, particularly in non-ambulant girls. The severity of scoliosis was associated with a poor prognosis and life expectancy; thus, in individuals with early onset scoliosis, a surgical approach could be considered in order to improve the frequency of severe respiratory tract infections also (Downs et al., 2016b).

Some studies evidenced abnormal electrocardiographic findings in RTT patients, such as a prolongation of QT corrected interval, tachycardia, bradycardia, and atrioventricular block; sudden cardiac death was also reported in young patients (Acampa & Guideri, 2006).

As pleomorphic features, these patients show autonomic dysregulation, leading to abnormal breathing patterns. Hyperventilation or breath-holding are common clinical manifestations of this autonomic dysfunction (Julu et al., 2001; Weese-Mayer et al., 2006). Abdominal bloating, which in rare cases can lead to gastric perforation, is a common sequela and may need alleviation through the release of air via a gastrostomy (Baikie et al., 2014).

1.2.3 Sleep disturbance

Other symptoms are related to sleep, and sleep disturbances have recently even been considered as supportive criteria for RTT (Hagberg et al., 2002; Neul, 2010). Low nighttime sleep and daytime naps have been described in the RTT patients although night laughing and screaming usually decreased over time (Ellaway et al., 2001; Young et al., 2007; Wong et al., 2015). A higher prevalence of somnolence has been reported in patients showing epilepsy or impaired mobility. A link with Arg294X or large deletion was associated with increased risk of sleep disturbances, and particularly with initiating and maintaining sleep (Boban et al., 2016).

In accordance with a mouse model showing that MeCP2 deficiency is associated with lower bone strength, in subjects with RTT, fracture risk was observed to be four times higher than in the general female population, and was specifically increased in those with Arg168X and Arg270X mutations (O'Connor et al., 2009; Kamal et al., 2015; Downs et al., 2008). Poor vitamin D status and other known fracture risk factors, possibly genotype or the use of certain anti-epileptic medications, correlate with low bone mineral density (Leonard et al., 2010; Catalano, 2016, 2017, 2018).

In conclusion, we suggest to parents and professionals to carefully observe the child's growth and development and the presence of certain core symptoms for typical RTT, such as: partial or complete loss of acquired purposeful hand skills and spoken language; gait abnormalities; and stereotypic hand movements. If they think they identify any of the comorbidities, we suggest looking for the presence of scoliosis, because it is the most prevalent orthopedic comorbidity. Moreover, we recommend paying attention if a deceleration of postnatal head growth occurs, because it is often a sign that initially alerts professionals to RTT as a potential diagnosis.

1.3 Stages of development in RTT

Overall, RTT life course is commonly divided into four stages:

Stage I: early onset. Signs and symptoms which start between 6 and 18 months of age are subtle and easily overlooked; young patients lose interest in playing with toys and show less eye contact or delays in sitting or crawling.

Stage II: rapid destruction. Over a period between one and four years of age, children lose the ability to perform skills they previously had, and manifestations of RTT including abnormal hand movements, hyperventilating, crying for no apparent reason, and a loss of social interaction, clearly appear.

Stage III: plateau. Until ten years of age, although movement disorders persist, behavior may improve, with less crying and irritability, and some improvement in hand use and communication. At this stage, seizures may begin; however, this is usually not before the age of two.

Stage IV: late motor deterioration. High muscle weakness, reduced mobility, multiple articular impairment, and scoliosis are evident after the first decade and may cause pain; however, communication problems may prevent others from recognizing pain.

1.4 Revision of the diagnostic criteria

The diverse and complicated clinical phenotype of RTT has resulted in a revision of the clinical diagnostic criteria over the years to facilitate the identification of typical and atypical RTT cases (Gold et al., 2018).

The *Diagnostic and Statistical Manual of Mental Disorders* (DSM-5, American Psychiatric Association, 2013) is the most comprehensive, current, and critical resource for the diagnosis and classification of mental disorders. The DSM-5 is used by clinicians and researchers to diagnose and classify mental disorders and is the product of more than ten years of effort by hundreds of international experts in all aspects of mental health.

The release of the DSM-5 has provided a significant change for the diagnosis and classification of RTT. In the previous version of the DSM, RTT had been classified as one form of five distinct categories of autism-related disorders. In the current edition, RTT was removed. The decision to remove RTT as a unique diagnosis within the DSM-5 was the result of much research and consideration; however, its exclusion does not negate the importance of the disorder on those directly affected by it (Clark, 2015).

The Neul (2010) criteria are now the diagnostic criteria most commonly used for the identification of new cases of RTT (see Table 1.1).

According to the International Rett Syndrome Foundation (2014), individuals who meet any of the following criteria can be excluded from a classic RTT diagnosis: (1) traumatic brain injury; (2) neuro-metabolic disease; (3) neurological problems caused by a severe infection; and (4) significant abnormalities in gross development prior to the child reaching six months of age. If none of these criteria apply to the individual, and the child has been identified to have had a period of regression accompanied by a period of stabilization, the physician will then review whether the child meets the main criteria for diagnosis. These criteria include: (1) partial or complete loss of acquired purposeful hand skills; (2) partial or complete loss of spoken language acquisition; (3) abnormalities of gait; and (4) stereotypic repetitive hand movements, which must all be present to indicate an RTT diagnosis (Neul, 2010). Moreover, the supportive criteria, which include scoliosis, breathing problems when awake, abnormal sleep patterns, inappropriate laughing, and diminished response to pain, provide more symptoms that may be evident in some, but not all, of those with RTT and are therefore not required components of the diagnosis.

1.5 Conclusion

As discussed in this chapter, RTT is a complex syndrome characterized by a broad clinical spectrum of signs and symptoms and a peculiar course. This disorder affects different systems: nervous, musculo-skeletal, gastro-enteric. Loss of purposeful hand movements and speech and regression of acquired cognitive and motor skills are the core symptoms associated with RTT. Management of symptoms and health-related problems may require a multispecialty team that should propose follow-up, possibly preserving quality of life, by preventing or delaying the consequences of RTT. Treatments and management will be the topics of the next chapter.

References

Acampa, M. & Guideri, F. (2006). Cardiac disease and Rett syndrome. *Archives of Disease in Childhood*, 91(5), 440–443.

Adachi, M., Autry, A.E., Herb, E.C. & Monteggia, L.M. (2009). MeCP2-mediated transcription repression in the basolateral amygdala may underlie heightened anxiety in a mouse model of Rett syndrome. *Journal of Neurosciences*, 29, 4218–4227.

Aldenkamp, A.P. & Arends, J. (2004). Effects of epileptiform EEG discharges on cognitive function: is the concept of "transient cognitive impairment" still valid? *Epilepsy Behavior*, 5(1), 25–34.

American Psychiatric Association (2013). *Diagnostic and Statistical Manual of Mental Disorders* (5th ed.). Arlington, VA: American Psychiatric Publishing.

Anderson, A., Wong, K., Jacoby, P., Downs, J. & Leonard, H. (2014). Twenty years of surveillance in Rett syndrome: what does this tell us? *Orphanet Journal of Rare Disorders*, 9, 87.

Baikie, G. et al. (2014). Gastrointestinal dysmotility in Rett syndrome. *Journal of Pediatriac Gastroenterology Nutrition*, 58, 237–244.

Bao, X., Downs, J., Wong, K., Williams, S. & Leonard, H. (2013). Using a large international sample to investigate epilepsy in Rett syndrome. *Developmental Medicine & Child Neurology*, 55, 553–558.

Bebbington, A. et al. (2008). Investigating genotype–phenotype relationships in Rett syndrome using an international data set. *Neurology*, 70, 868–875.

Boban, S. et al. (2016). Determinants of sleep disturbances in Rett syndrome: novel findings in relation to genotype. *American Journal of Medical Genetics*, 170, 2292–2300.

Catalano, A. (2016). Effects of teriparatide on bone mineral density and quality of life in Duchenne muscular dystrophy related osteoporosis: a case report. *Osteoporos International*, 27(12), 3655–3659.

Catalano, A. et al. (2017). Pain in osteoporosis: from pathophisiology to therapeutic approach. *Drugs and Aging*, *34*(10), 755–765.

Catalano, A. et al. (2018). Anxiety levels predict fracture risk in postmenopausal women assessed for osteoporosis. *Menopause 25*(10), 1110–1115.

Downs, J. et al. (2008). Early determinants of fractures in Rett syndrome. *Pediatrics*, *121*, 540–546.

Downs, J. et al. (2010). Level of purposeful hand function as a marker of clinical severity in Rett syndrome. *Developmental Medicine & Child Neurology*, *52*, 817–823.

Downs, J. et al. (2016a). Validating the Rett Syndrome Gross Motor Scale. *PLoS ONE*, *11*, e0147555.

Downs, J. et al. (2016b). Surgical fusion of early onset severe scoliosis increases survival in Rett syndrome: a cohort study. *Developmental Medicine & Child Neurology*, *58*, 632–638.

Ellaway, C., Peat, J., Leonard, H. & Christodoulou, J. (2001). Sleep dysfunction in Rett syndrome: lack of age related decrease in sleep duration. *Brain and Development*, *23*, S101–S103.

Fabio, R.A., Giannatiempo, S., Antonietti, A. & Budden, S. (2009). The role of stereotypies in overselectivity processes in Rett Sindrome. *Research in Developmental Disabilities*, *30*, 136–145.

Fehr, S. et al. (2011). Altered attainment of developmental milestones influences the age of diagnosis of Rett syndrome. *Journal of Child Neurology*, *26*, 980–987.

Foley, K.R. et al. (2011). Change in gross motor abilities of girls and women with Rett syndrome over a 3- to 4-year period. *Journal of Child Neurology*, *26*, 1237–1245.

Glaze, D.G., Frost, J.D. Jr, Zoghbi, H.Y. & Percy, A.K. (1987). Rett's syndrome. Correlation of electroencephalographic characteristics with clinical staging. *Archives of Neurology*, *44*, 1053–1056.

Glaze, D.G., Schultz, R.J. & Frost, J.D. (1998). Rett syndrome: characterization of seizures versus nonseizures. *Electroencephalography and Clinical Neurophysiology*, *106*, 79–83.

Glaze, D.G. et al. (2010). Epilepsy and the natural history of Rett syndrome. *Neurology*, *74*, 909–912.

Gold W. A., Krishnarajy R., Ellaway C. & Christodoulou J. (2018). Rett syndrome: A genetic update and clinical review focusing on comorbidities. *ACS Chemical Neuroscience*, *9*(2), 167–176.

Goutières, F. & Aicardi, J. (1986). Atypical forms of Rett syndrome. *American Journal of Medical Genetics*, *1*, 183–194.

Hagberg, B., Aicardi, J., Dias, K. & Ramos, O. (1983). A progressive syndrome of autism, dementia, ataxia, and loss of purposeful hand use in girls: Rett's syndrome: report of 35 cases. *Annals of Neurology*, *14*, 471–479.

Hagberg, B., Goutières, F., Hanefeld, F., Rett, A. & Wilson, J. (1985). Rett syndrome: criteria for inclusion and exclusion. *Brain and Development*, *7*, 372–373.

Hagberg, B., Hanefeld, F., Percy, A. & Skjeldal, O. (2002). An update on clinically applicable diagnostic criteria in Rett syndrome. Comments to Rett Syndrome Clinical Criteria Consensus Panel Satellite to European Paediatric Neurology Society Meeting, Baden Baden, Germany, 11 September 2001. *European Journal of Paediatriac Neurology*, 6, 293–297.

Hagberg, B.A. & Skjeldal, O.H. (1994). Rett variants: a suggested model for inclusion criteria. *Pediatriac Neurology*, 11, 5–11.

Jian, L. et al. (2006). Predictors of seizure onset in Rett syndrome. *Journal of Pediatry*, 149, 542–547.

Jian, L. et al. (2007a). Seizures in Rett syndrome: an overview from a one-year calendar study. *European Journal of Paediatriac Neurology*, 11, 310–317.

Jian, L., Nagarajan, L., de Klerk, N., Ravine, D., Christodoulou, J. & Leonard, H. (2007b). Seizures in Rett syndrome: an overview from a 1-year calendar study. *European Journal of Paediatriac Neurology*, 11, 310–317.

Julu, P.O. et al. (2001). Characterisation of breathing and associated central autonomic dysfunction in the Rett disorder. *Archives of Disease in Childhood*, 85, 29–37.

Kaaden, S. & Helmstaedter, C. (2009). Age at onset of epilepsy as a determinant of intellectual impairment in temporal lobe epilepsy. *Epilepsy Behaviour*, 15, 213–217.

Kamal, B. et al. (2015). Biomechanical properties of bone in a mouse model of Rett syndrome. *Bone*, 71, 106–114.

Lang, M. et al. (2014). Rescue of behavioral and EEG deficits in male and female Mecp2-deficient mice by delayed Mecp2gene reactivation. *Human Molecular Genetics*, 23, 303–318.

Lee, J.Y., Leonard, H., Piek, J.P. & Downs, J. (2013). Early development and regression in Rett syndrome. *Clinical Genetics*, 84, 572–576.

Leonard, H. & Bower, C. (1998). Is the girl with Rett syndrome normal at birth? *Developmental Medicine and Child Neurology*, 40, 115–121.

Leonard, H. et al. (2010).Valproate and risk of fracture in Rett syndrome. *Archives of Disease in Childhood*, 95, 444–448.

Meletti, S., Benuzzi, F., Cantalupo, G., Rubboli, G., Tassinari, C. A. & Nichelli, P. (2009). Facial emotion recognition impairment in chronic temporal lobe epilepsy. *Epilepsia*, 50(6), 1547–1559.

Neul, J.L. (2010). Rett syndrome: revised diagnostic criteria and nomenclature. *Annals of Neurology*, 68, 944–950.

Nissenkorn, A. et al. (2015). Epilepsy in Rett syndrome – lessons from the Rett networked database. *Epilepsia*, 56, 569–576.

O'Connor, R.D., Zayzafoon, M., Farach-Carson, M.C. & Schanen, N.C. (2009). Mecp2 deficiency decreases bone formation and reduces bone volume in a rodent model of Rett syndrome. *Bone*, 45, 346–356.

Percy, A.K. et al. (2010). Profiling scoliosis in Rett syndrome. *Pediatriac Research*, 67, 435–439.

Rett, A. (1966). On a unusual brain atrophy syndrome in hyperammonemia in childhood. *Wien Med Wochenschr*, 116, 723–726.

Steffenburg, U., Hagberg, G. & Hagberg, B. (2001). Epilepsy in a representative series of Rett syndrome. *Acta Paediatrics*, *90*, 34–39.

Tarquinio, D.C. et al. (2012). Growth failure and outcome in Rett syndrome: specific growth references. *Neurology*, *79*, 1653–1661.

Trevathan, E. (1989). Rett syndrome. *Pediatrics*, *83*, 636–637.

Urbanowicz, A., Downs, J., Girdler, S., Ciccone, N. & Leonard, H. (2015). Aspects of speech–language abilities are influenced by MECP2mutation type in girls with Rett syndrome. *American Journal of Medical Genetics*, *167*, 354–362.

Vignoli, A., Fabio, R.A., La Briola, F., Giannatiempo, S., Antonietti, A., Maggiolini, S. & Canevini, M.P. (2010). Correlations between neurophysiological, behavioral, and cognitive function in Rett syndrome. *Epilepsy and Behavior*, *17*(4), 489–496.

Wong, K., Leonard, H., Jacoby, P., Ellaway, C. & Downs, J. (2015). The trajectories of sleep disturbances in Rett syndrome. *Journal of Sleep Research*, *24*, 223–233.

Young, D. et al. (2007). Sleep problems in Rett syndrome. *Brain and Development*, *29*, 609–616.

Zappella, M. (1992). The Rett girls with preserved speech. *Brain and Development*, *14*, 98–101.

Chapter 2

What causes Rett Syndrome

Rett Syndrome (RTT) is a complex genetic disorder. Parents of children who receive a diagnosis of RTT feel scared, confused, frustrated, angry, or uncertain, and their emotions may change from day to day.

Anna, the mother of Silvia says:

> "I expected the test to come back positive, but hearing the doctor say the words still left me devastated. My beautiful flower, my blue flower (her eyes are colored blue like a periwinkle) had Rett Syndrome. I was so profoundly sad, scared and dejected. And also very angry".

Professionals can help parents by explaining to them that although at the moment there is no cure for this syndrome, treatment is directed toward symptoms and providing support, which may improve the potential for movement, communication, and social participation. They have to explain that the need for treatment and support doesn't end as children become older – it's usually necessary throughout life.

Professionals have also to explain that all girls with RTT have a very high potential to learn, both in the cognitive field and the motor field. Modifiability is always possible, even when the symptoms are extremely severe. With the correct interventions, they can also live and enjoy a good quality of life.

In this chapter, we offer a detailed scientific explanation of RTT. If the reader is a parent, he or she can skip the details and move on to Chapter 3 concerning how to manage the condition.

RTT is a neurodevelopmental disorder caused by a mutation in the X-linked gene encoding for methyl-CpG-binding protein 2 (MeCP2). Genotype and severity of RTT symptoms have been found to be related, affecting the amplitude of comorbidities. How the gene mutation observed affects various biological processes on multiple levels will be illustrated in the first part of the chapter – although how the effects of gene mutation on the phenotype are mediated at the molecular level is not yet known. The second part will deal with the multifactorial features of the syndrome, leading to considering phenotype relapses which seem to be wide, as opposed to the apparent univocality of the gene anomaly. The neurobiology of MeCP2 will be looked at in the third part, with regard to the fact that the loss of MeCP2 disrupts the given brain region or system from which it is deleted, and that localized disruption results in a subset of commonly observed symptoms of common RTT.

2.1 The causes of RTT

As seen in Chapter 1, RTT is characterized by neurological impairment that leads to a dramatic deficit of normal age-related functions (Neul, 2010; Percy et al., 2010) and it is caused by inactivating mutations in the X-linked gene encoding for a regulator of epigenetic gene expression, methyl-CpG-binding protein 2 (MeCP2) (Amir et al., 1999; Evans & Meyer, 1999).

The MeCP2 gene is located on the long (q) arm of the X chromosome in band 28 ("Xq28"), from base pair 152,808,110 to base pair 152,878,611 (McGraw et al., 2011; Villard, 2007).

MeCP2 has been previously classified as a molecule which interacts with DNA bearing methylated cytosines in the context of CpG dinucleotides (Kumar et al., 2008; Nan et al., 1996; Lewis et al., 1992). The aminoterminal disrupting methyl-CpG-binding domain (MBD) mediates the association of MeCP2 with densely methylated heterochromatic foci in mouse fibroblasts, suggesting that it is a functional protein domain in vivo, and mutations in this domain of MeCP2 cause decreased residence time at heterochromatic foci (Mullaney et al., 2004).

At a nuclear level, it has been proposed that MeCP2 compacts chromatin structure and represses transcription by recruiting, as in a bridge model, the nuclear receptor co-repressor–silencing mediator of retinoic acid and thyroid hormone receptor (NCOR–SMRT) co-repressor complex, or activates transcription by recruiting the co-activator cyclic AMP-responsive elementbinding protein 1 (CREB1) (Lyst et al., 2013; Nan et al., 1997).

Mutations can disrupt the bridge through impaired binding to DNA by mutations that disrupt the methyl-CpG-binding domain (MBD) function, by truncating MeCP2 upstream of the NCOR–SMRT inter-action domain (Chen et al., 2001). Here following, the scheme of the MeCP2 gene with its four exons and functional domains NTS, MBD, ID, TRD is reported:

> In the chromatin compaction model, MeCP2 regulates chromatin architecture by interacting with the genome through its different DNA-binding domains. Loss of the NID (for example, the R306C or G273X mutations) impair MeCP2 function regarding chroma-tin organization, although binding to DNA is partially preserved.
> (Baker et al., 2013)

Earlier truncation mutation, which also abolishes an AT-hook motif (R270X), MeCP2, binds to DNA without being able to induce mod-ification of the chromatin structure. This kind of R270X mutation provokes a more severe disease phenotype in humans and in animal models in comparison with G273X or R306C (Baker et al., 2013).

The relevant role of MeCP2 in the organization of chromatin architecture is highlighted by ectopic expression of MeCP2 through transient transfection of mouse myoblasts that resulted in clustering of chromo centers and by the loss of a chromatin loop in MeCP2-knockout mice (Samaco et al., 2013). In addition, a similar effect was observed with recombinant MeCP2 that is able to bind to and com-pact nucleosomal arrays (Georgel et al., 2003; Nikitina et al., 2006).

MeCP2 was able to compete with histone H1, and MeCP2 null mice display increased levels of histone H1. These results suggest that displacement of histone H1 could reveal a mechanism which leads MeCP2 to modulate higher-order chromatin architecture, probably to regulate gene expression.

At a molecular level, MeCP2 could regulate an alternative splicing through the interaction with Y-box transcription factor (YB1); fur-thermore, it could regulate microRNA (miRNA) processing by inter-acting with DiGeorge syndrome chromosomal region 8 (DGCR8) to prevent the formation of the Drosha–DGCR8 complex (Maunakea et al., 2013; Cheng et al., 2014)

MeCP2 might also serve to regulate gene expression at a post-transcriptional level. MeCP2 also interacts with many proteins, includ-ing chromatin modifying factors (Chahrour et al., 2008).

In brains from MeCP2 null mice compared with wild mice, gene expression profiling at the beginning failed to reveal differences in gene expression patterns; later, considering specific brain regions in

MeCP2 null mice and in mice overexpressing MeCP2, it was detected that gene expression was significantly dysregulated, with more genes being downregulated than unregulated in the absence of MeCP2. Thus, the majority of MePC2 controlled genes are positively regulated by MeCP2 (Guy et al., 2001, 2007; Chahrour et al., 2008).

The major evidence on MeCP2 and RETT pathophysiology comes from patient-derived cells and genetically modified mice, including MeCP2-knockout lines.

Experimental studies have been carried out with MeCP2-knockout models in which the gene had been deleted from specific brain regions or brain cell types, or at different stages of development.

The reversibility of the RTT-like phenotype upon restoration of MeCP2 activity and the dramatic consequences of the loss of function of MeCP2 in adult mice argues that MeCP2 seems to be required for the lifelong maintenance of physiological neuronal function (Cheval et al., 2012; Nguyen et al., 2012).

Deletion of MeCP2 from glial cells has mild phenotypic consequences, and this finding supports a main role of MeCP2 in neurons. However, a significant increase in lifespan has been reported when MeCP2 is expressed specifically in oligodendrocytes of MeCP2 null mice. MeCP2 function is therefore not restricted to neuronal cells (Lioy et al., 2011; Derecki et al., 2012).

Observations made using animal models should be considered with caution because they could introduce some potential caveats: hemizygous MeCP2 null male mice are frequently used, but the most direct representation of patients with RTT would be MeCP2 heterozygous female mice. Moreover, symptoms of MeCP2 deficiency in mice models, including an abnormal gait, breathing disturbances, and premature lethality in males, appear at a later stage in the development than in humans (Villard, 2007).

As mentioned previously, experiments on MeCP2 have been carried out focusing on MeCP2 deletion in specific brain regions and neuronal subtypes in mice. It has been noted that loss of MeCP2 in a specific domain compromises the function of the related brain region (Kumar et al., 2008). The forebrain MeCP2 deletion causes behavioral abnormalities such as limb clasping, impaired motor coordination, increased anxiety, and abnormal social behavior, but does not affect locomotor activity or context-dependent fear conditioning, the control of which resides elsewhere in the brain (Lioy et al., 2011).

Similarly, loss of MeCP2 from all inhibitory gamma-Aminobutyric acid (GABA) releasing neurons leads to a severe RTT-like phenotype, whereas a smaller subset of MeCP2 negative neurons has much milder consequences (Chao et al., 2010).

It is known that changes in gene expression of mouse models of RTT induce phenotypic modifications, and the overall effect of such changes could explain, at least in part, the pathology of RTT (Ben-Shachar et al., 2009).

Some lines of evidence suggest that MeCP2 target genes may be expressed at different levels in mice carrying mutations of MeCP2. Corticotropin releasing hormone (Crh) and opioid receptor mu-1 (Oprm1) are two genes linked to anxiety behavior; their expression has been upregulated in mice overexpressing MeCP2, and lowering their expression produced a modification of the anxiety phenotype observed in those animals (Samaco et al., 2013).

Moreover, levels of the brain-derived neurotrophic factor (BDNF), an autocrine factor that promotes neuronal growth and survival, are lower in MeCP2 null mice; conversely, the overexpression of BDNF in MeCP2 null mice improves phenotype and survival (Chang et al., 2006).

Human observations allow us to understand that the nature of the MeCP2 mutation affects RTT severity; it is also possible to examine a broad spectrum of disease-causing MeCP2 mutations since large patient databases such as RettBASE are now available (Cuddapah et al., 2014).

Recently, it has been discovered that variants which were previously called "congenital" or "early onset epilepsy" are caused by different mutations. It is now established that the "congenital" variant, also called the "Hanefeld variant", is caused by the mutation FOXG1, while the variant with early onset of epilepsy is connected to the mutation CDKL5; however, CDKL5 disorder seems to be an independent clinical entity from RTT, although they may be related (Ariani et al., 2008; Pini et al., 2012; Rajaei et al., 2011).

The commonly deleted region includes the telomeric breakpoint of the inversion in the latter patient and contains FOXG1, a strong candidate gene based on high and specific expression in the developing brain, and complex malformations of the telencephalon in both homozygous and heterozygous mouse mutants (Eagleson et al., 2007).

Recently, duplications of FOXG1 have been associated with developmental epilepsy, intellectual disability (ID), and severe speech impairment in eight patients (Brunetti-Pierri et al., 2011).

There are three types of mutations in FOXG1 associated with RTT; partial or total duplication of the gene, deletion of the gene, and less frequently, a truncation misspelling, which is a premature stop in the spelling of the gene. The severity of symptoms seems to vary among the different mutations from mild to severe.

2.2 Genotype–phenotype correlation

Several studies have reported a relationship between some characteristics of the phenotype and the genotype, but patients with the same MeCP2 mutation can vary greatly in phenotype, so there may be other mechanisms modulating the clinical presentation (Fabio et al., 2018; Falzone et al., 2015; Vignoli et al., 2010; Weaving et al., 2005). With respect to neurodevelopmental and behavioral phenotypes, girls affected by RTT vary, and the reason for the differences is not well understood. Moreover, the clinical and electroencephalographic (EEG) picture of girls with RTT follows different stages correlated with age (Glaze, 2002), and EEG patterns vary not only between patients, but also between stages of the disease (Buoni et al., 2008; Moser et al., 2007).

A study by Fabio and colleagues (2014) evaluated a cohort of 114 RTT patients with a detailed scale measuring the different kinds of impairments produced by the syndrome. The sample included relatively large subsets of the most frequent mutations, so that genotype–phenotype correlations could be tested. Results revealed that frequent missense mutations showed a specific profile in different areas of impairment. The R306C mutation, considered as one producing mild impairment, was associated with a moderate phenotype in which behavioral characteristics were mainly affected. A notable difference emerged by comparing mutations truncating the protein before and after the nuclear localization signal; such a difference generally concerned the motorfunctional and autonomy skills of the patients, affecting the management of everyday activities.

Overall, the most important innovation introduced in the study of Fabio and colleagues (2014) was the use of a set of fine-grained measures to assess the level of severity of the RTT symptoms. Most of the previous studies assessed the phenotypic features of RTT patients mainly through a few indices, global evaluation, or qualitative descriptions, which are associated with extensive subjectivity.

2.3 Conclusions

It is well known that mutations in MeCP2 cause RTT. The clinical picture of RTT appears quite heterogeneous for every single feature.

Mutations in the MeCP2 gene have been associated with the onset of RTT. However, other mutations have been correlated to RTT, such as CDLK5 and FOXG1. For example, there is a cohort of RTT patients which does not fit into the "classical" form and has been grouped according to an atypical RTT phenotype which is characterized by the age of the regression onset (frusta form, late regression onset, neonatal encephalopathy) or by the presence of verbal speech (Preserved Speech Variant).

In conclusion, considering this range of behavioral patterns, it is important to analyze if specific phenotypic symptoms in RTT are related to specific genotypes, although the mutation in MeCP2 is the main cause of RTT.

References

Amir, R.E., VandenVeyver, I.B., Wan, M., Tran, C.Q., Francke, U. & Zoghbi, H.Y. (1999). Rett syndrome is caused by mutations in X-linked MeCP2, encoding methyl-CpG-binding protein2. *Nature Genetics, 23,* 185–188.

Ariani, F. et al. (2008). FOXG1 is responsible for the congenital variant of rett syndrome. *American Journal of Human Genetics, 83,* 89–93.

Baker, S.A., Chen, L., Wilkins, A.D., Yu, P., Lichtarge, O. & Zoghbi, H.Y. (2013). An AT-hook domain in MeCP2 determines the clinical course of Rett syndrome and related disorders. *Cell, 152,* 984–996.

Ben-Shachar, S., Chahrour, M., Thaller, C., Shaw, C.A. & Zoghbi, H.Y. (2009). Mouse models of MeCP2 disorders share gene expression changes in the cerebellum and hypothalamus. *Human Molecular Genetics, 18*(13), 2431–2442.

Brunetti-Pierri, N. et al. (2011). Duplications of *FOXG1* in 14q12 are associated with developmental epilepsy, mental retardation, and severe speech impairment. *European Journal of Human Genetics, 19,* 102–107.

Buoni, S. et al. (2008). Drug-resistant epilepsy and epileptic phenotype–EEG association in MECP2 mutated Rett syndrome. *Clinical Neurophysiology, 119,* 2455–2458.

Chahrour, M. et al. (2008). MeCP2, a key contributor to neurological disease, activates and represses transcription. *Science, 320,* 1224–1229.

Chang, Q., Khare, G., Dani, V., Nelson, S. & Jaenisch, R. (2006). The disease progression of Mecp2 mutant mice is affected by the level of BDNF expression. *Neuron, 49,* 341–348.

Chao, H.T., Chen, H., Samaco, R.C., Xue, M., Chahrour, M., Yoo, J., Neul, J.L., Gong, S., Lu, H.C., Heintz, N., Ekker, M., Rubenstein, J.L., Noebels, J.L., Rosenmund, C. & Zoghbi, H.Y. (2010). Dysfunction in GABA signalling mediates autism-like stereotypies and rett syndrome phenotypes. *Nature, 468,* 263–269.

Chen, R.Z., Akbarian, S., Tudor, M. & Jaenisch, R. (2001). Deficiency of methyl-Cpg binding protein-2 in CNS neurons results in a Rett-like phenotype in mice. *Nature Genetics, 27*, 327–331.

Cheng, T.L. et al. (2014). MeCP2 suppresses nuclear microRNA processing and dendritic growth by regulating the DGCR8/Drosha complex. *Developmental Cell, 28*, 547–560.

Cheval, H., Guy, J., Merusi, C., De Sousa, D., Selfridge, J. & Bird, A. (2012). Postnatal inactivation reveals enhanced requirement for MeCP2 at distinct age windows. *Human Molecular Genetics, 21*, 3806–3814.

Cuddapah, V.A. et al. (2014). Methyl-CpG-binding protein 2 (*MECP2*) mutation type is associated with disease severity in Rett syndrome. *Journal of Medical Genetics, 51*, 152–158.

Derecki, N.C., Cronk, J.C., Lu, Z., Xu, E., Abbott, S.B., Guyenet, P.G. & Kipnis, J. (2012). Wild-type microglia arrest pathology in a mouse model of Rett syndrome. *Nature, 484*, 105–109.

Eagleson, K.L., Schlueter, L.J., McFadyen-Ketchum, E.T., Ahrens, P.H., Mills, M.D., Does, J. & Levitt, N.P. (2007). Disruption of Foxg1 expression by knock-in of Cre recombinase: effects on the development of the mouse telencephalon. *Neuroscience, 148*(2), 385–395.

Evans, I.M. & Meyer, L.M. (1999). Modifying adult interactional style as positive behavioural intervention for a child with Rett syndrome. *Journal of Intellectual Developmental Disabilities, 24*, 191–205.

Fabio, R.A., Colombo, B., Russo, S., Cogliati, S.F, Masciandri, M., Antonietti, A. & Tavian, D. (2014). Recent insights into genotype-phenotype relationships in patients with Rett syndrome using a fine grain scale. *Research in Developmental Disabilities, 35*(11), 2976–2986.

Fabio, R.A., Caprì, T., Lotan, M., Towey, G.E. & Martino, G. (2018). Motor abilities are related to the specific genotype in Rett Syndrome. In *Advances in Genetic Research*, vol. 18, chapter id 32719, 79–108. New York: Nova Science Publisher.

Falzone, A., Gangemi, A. & Fabio, R.A. (2015). Genotype-phenotype relationships in language processes in Rett syndrome. In *Advances in Genetic Research*, vol. 14, chapter id 32719. New York: Nova Science Publisher.

Glaze, D.G. (2002). Neurophysiology of Rett Syndrome. *Mental Retardation and Developmental Disabilities Research Reviews, 8*, 66–71.

Georgel, P.T., Horowitz-Scherer, R.A., Adkins, N., Woodcock, C.L., Wade, P.A. & Hansen, J.C. (2003). Chromatin compaction by human MeCP2. Assembly of novel secondary chromatin structures in the absence of DNA methylation. *Journal of Biological Chemistry, 278*, 32181–32188.

Guy, J., Hendrich, B., Holmes, M., Martin, J.E. & Bird, A. (2001). A mouse Mecp2-null mutation causes neurological symptoms that mimic Rett Syndrome. *Nature Genetics, 27*, 322–326.

Guy, J., Gan, J., Selfridge, J., Cobb, S. & Bird, A. (2007). Reversal of neurological defects in a mouse model of Rett Syndrome. *Science, 315*, 1143–1147.

Kumar, A., Kamboj, S., Malone, B.M., Kudo, S., Twiss, J.L., Czymmek, K.J., LaSalle, J.M. & Schanen, N.C. (2008). Analysis of protein domains and Rett syndrome mutations indicate that multiple regions influence chromatin-binding dynamics of the chromatin-associated protein MeCP2 in vivo. *Journal of Cell Science*, *121*, 1128–1137.

Lewis, J.D., Meehan, R.R., Henzel, W.J., Maurer-Fogy, I., Jeppesen, P., Klein, F. & Bird, A. (1992). Purification, sequence, and cellular localization of a novel chromosomal protein that binds to methylated DNA. *Cell*, *69*, 905–914.

Lioy, D.T., Garg, S.K., Monaghan, C.E., Raber, J., Foust, K.D., Kaspar, B.K. & Hirrlinger, P.G., Kirchhoff, F., Bissonnette, J.M., Ballas, N. & Mandel, G. (2011). A role for glia in the progression of Rett's syndrome. *Nature*, *475*, 497–500.

Lyst, M.J. et al. (2013). Rett syndrome mutations abolish the interaction of MeCP2 with the NCoR/SMRT co-repressor. *Nature Neuroscience*, *16*, 898–902.

Maunakea, A.K. et al. (2013). Intragenic DNA methylation modulates alternative splicing by recruiting MeCP2 to promote exon recognition. *Cell Research*, *23*, 1256–1269.

McGraw, C.M., Samaco R.C. & Zoghbi, H.Y. (2011). Adult neural function requires MeCP2. *Science*, *333*, 186.

Moser, S.J., Weber, P. & Lütschg, J. (2007). Rett syndrome: clinical and electrophysiologic aspects. *Pediatric Neurology*, *36*, 95–100.

Mullaney, B.C., Johnston, M.V. & Blue, M.E. (2004). Developmental expression of methyl-CpG binding protein 2 is dynamically regulated in the rodent brain. *Neuroscience*, *123*, 939–949.

Nan, X., Campoy, F.J. & Bird, A. (1997). MeCP2 is a transcriptional repressor with abundant binding sites in genomic chromatin. *Cell*, *88*, 471–481.

Nan, X., Tate, P., Li, E. & Bird, A. (1996). DNA methylation specifies chromosomal localization of MeCP2. *Molecular and Cellular Biology*, *16*, 414–421.

Neul, J.L. (2010). Rett syndrome: revised diagnostic criteria and nomenclature. *Annals of Neurology*, *68*, 944–950.

Nguyen, M.V., Du, F., Felice, C.A., Shan, X., Nigam, A., Mandel, G., Robinson, J.K. & Ballas, N. (2012). MeCP2 is critical for maintaining mature neuronal networks and global brain anatomy during late stages of postnatal brain development and in the mature adult brain. *Journal of Neuroscience*, *32*, 10021–10034.

Nikitina, T., Shi, X., Ghosh, R.P., Horowitz-Scherer, R.A., Hansen, J.C. & Woodcock, C.L. (2006). Multiple modes of interaction between the methylated DNA binding protein MeCP2 and chromatin. *Molecular Cellular and Biology*, *27*(3), 864–877.

Percy, A.K. et al. (2010). Profiling scoliosis in Rett syndrome. *Pediatriac Research*, *67*, 435–439.

Pini, G. et al. (2012). Variant of rett syndrome and CDKL5 gene: clinical and autonomic description of 10 cases. *Neuropediatrics*, *43*, 37–43.

Rajaei, S. et al. (2011). Early infantile onset "Congenital" Rett syndrome variants: Swedish experience through four decades and mutation analysis. *Journal of Child Neurology*, 26, 65–71.

Samaco, R.C., McGraw, C.M., Ward, C.S., Sun, Y., Neul, J.L. & Zoghbi, H.Y. (2013) Female Mecp2+/– mice display robust behavioral deficits on two different genetic backgrounds providing a framework for pre-clinical studies. *Humuna Molecule Genetic*, 22, 96–109.

Vignoli, A., Fabio, R.A., La Briola, F., Giannatiempo, S., Antonietti, A, Maggiolini, S. & Canevini, M.P. (2010). Correlations between neurophysiological, behavioral, and cognitive function in Rett syndrome. *Epilepsy & Behavior*, 17, 489–496.

Villard, L. (2007). MECP2 mutations in males. *Journal of Medical Genetics*, 44, 417–423.

Weaving, L.S., Ellaway, C.J., Gecz, J. & Christodoulou, J. (2005). Rett syndrome: clinical review and genetic update. *Journal of Medical Genetics*, 44, 1–7.

Chapter 3

Living with the condition of Rett Syndrome

Quality of life and family systems

As stated in Chapter 2, Rett Syndrome (RTT) is a complex genetic disorder. Treatments are directed toward symptoms and providing support, which may improve the potential for movement, communication, and social participation of subjects with RTT. Unfortunately, the need for treatment and support doesn't end as children become older – it's usually necessary throughout life. There are currently only a few attempts that have tried to halt or reverse the progression of the disease, and so management is mainly symptomatic and individualized. At this point in time, it is not possible to predict the therapeutic potential of gene therapy (such as the AVXS-201) for individuals with Rett Syndrome.

For these reasons, a dynamic multidisciplinary approach is the most effective, with specialists coming from different areas: medicine, psychology, social, educational, and occupational. Attention needs to be paid to mobility and to the development of effective communication strategies. It is also important to have psychosocial support for families. In this scenario, management and quality of life for patients and caregivers are key. Quality of life is a multidimensional phenomenon composed of core domains that are influenced by personal characteristics and environmental and contextual variables. Domains and specific indicators of quality of life have been identified and critically assessed. From a medical and sociological point of view, good quality of life consists of the patient having the ability to enjoy normal life activities. The evaluation and promotion of quality of life are essential both in psychological and medical care. Given the multiple disabilities of RTT, it is crucial to enhance quality of life with multilevel interventions, as some factors can seriously impair quality of life, whereas others can greatly improve it. The first part of this chapter will discuss the quality of life of the girls with RTT and their families. In the second part, practical ways to manage the condition in the family will be suggested.

In particular, we will discuss the reciprocal interaction between RTT and the family system. This relationship will be explained in light of the family systems theory (FST).

3.1 Living with RTT: Quality of life

Quality of life is experienced when a person's needs and wants are met and when one has the opportunity to pursue life enrichment in major life settings (Schalock et al., 2002). To date, it is possible to note that there is a growing interest in the quality of life of the girls with RTT and their caregivers. It is well known that RTT affects the living conditions of both patients and their families, given the severity of the syndrome. Thus, it is reasonable to assume that living with the condition of RTT can be hard.

Some studies have suggested that parents of girls with RTT experience more stress than controls and they show an elevated risk for depression and reduced health-related quality of life (Cianfaglione et al., 2017; Sarajlija et al., 2013). A recent work (Sarajlija et al., 2013) investigated the factors influencing health-related quality of life and depression in mothers who care for children with RTT in Serbia. It was found that the severity of the daughters' RTT behavioral phenotype predicted increased anxiety and stress for their mothers. Epstein and colleagues (2016) examined the quality of life in school-aged children with RTT, interviewing their parents. They identified ten important areas relating to quality of life: physical health, body pain and discomfort, behavioral and emotional well-being, communication skills, movement and mobility, social connectedness, variety of activities, provision of targeted services, stability of daily routines, and the natural environment. These results evidenced the importance of health, daily functioning, and participation in community activities for quality of life. Hence, it is important to involve the parents in the interventions related to the improvement of quality of life in order to understand the needs of their daughter and to be able to read her signals.

Individuals with RTT also experience specific behavioral indications of stress or anxiety, such as stereotyped hand movements. Although this type of movement is one of the defining features of RTT, some studies have suggested that hand stereotypies may increase or intensify in response to stress or arousal (Temudo et al., 2008). Differences were reported in the percentage of time that subjects with RTT engaged in hand stereotypies across social and non-social activities (Sigafoos et al., 2000). Similarly, Hetzroni and Rubin (2006) reported that females with RTT exhibited increased hand stereotypy in response to interruptions of familiar activities like watching television or listening to music, and Stasolla and Caffò (2013) reported decreases in hand stereotypy along with increases in indices of happiness associated with structured activities and environmental stimulation.

Recent studies have evaluated the quality of life in subjects with severe intellectual disabilities (ID) and their caregiver using questionnaires such as the Italian version of the Impact of Childhood Illness Scale, the Optum SF-36v2 Health Survey or the quality of life in subjects with severe intellectual disabilities (Parisi et al., 2016). These studies have demonstrated that RTT has a significant impact on both the child's development and on the entire family. The parents have especially recognized their difficulties in explaining their child's illness to others and to the child herself, probably because of the psychosocial implications of the illness. Also, they have claimed that the psychological, social, and practical difficulties of living with the condition of RTT are not completely understood by others (Esposito et al., 2013, 2014; Matson et al., 2008; Naidu et al., 2003).

With reference to siblings of children with RTT, the parents can explain to them the illness and its treatment. In this case, we suggest giving clear and honest answers to all questions in a way your child can understand. For many questions, there won't be easy answers. And you can't always promise that everything is going to be fine. If your child asks "why us?", you should offer an honest response, for example: "I don't know". Explain that no-one knows why the illness occurred and that there is no treatment. Depending on their ages and maturity level, visiting the hospital, meeting the physician staff, or accompanying their sibling with RTT to the clinic for treatments can help make the situation less frightening and more understandable. The siblings might also expect less time from parents; thus, it can help if parents reserve some special time for each sibling. It can occur that the siblings experience a sense of embarrassment and ostracism by their peers. In this case, it can help to practice a short script so they can explain their sister's conditions to friends or classmates. It is also important to ask for help from teachers. Due to the complicated nature of management of children with RTT, it is crucial that families reach a high level of adaptation to the continuing challenges they will face over a long period of time, because the need for treatment and support doesn't end as children become older; it is usually necessary throughout life.

With reference to caretaker wellbeing, the clinical features of RTT impact both patients' and caretakers' quality of life. Some studies have examined caretaker quality of life in connection to RTT, identifying characteristics that affect caretaker wellbeing (Laurvick et al., 2006; Sarajlija et al., 2013). Two studies assessed clinical measures for RTT, including MeCP2 mutation, epilepsy, musculoskeletal problems, fractures, breathing problems, sleeping problems, stereotyped behaviors, and movement, and other manifestations, including ambulation and feeding problems. However, in these two studies, the clinical severity was not assessed, whereas it was evaluated in the work of Killian and colleagues (2016). The authors hypothesized that more severe clinical features would negatively impact the caretakers' physical quality of life, but would positively impact caretakers' mental quality of life. They identified characteristics of caretakers' quality of life in connection with RTT and determined key predictors from the National Institutes of Health funded Natural History Study. Also, they analyzed the relationships of caretaker quality of life with both caretaker and child disease burden characteristics. The Optum SF-36v2 Health Survey was used to assess caretakers' physical and mental quality of life (higher scores indicate better quality of life). Their results indicated that caretakers' quality of life in RTT is similar to that for caretakers in other chronic diseases. In addition, the clinical characteristics of RTT significantly impact quality of life.

In accordance with the studies described previously, emotions represent a significant factor for improving both subjects with RTT and caretakers' quality of life. It is important to understand the quality of life of family members of patients with RTT so that appropriate strategies can be developed to meet their needs. These family members are often critical to successful patient care. As described previously, the literature only explored the impact of RTT on family members of patients, and much of the existing work regarding family members focused on family caregivers, often overlooking those who may not identify themselves as carers, but who live with or spend time with the patient and may still be greatly affected. Therefore, studies examining the quality of life of all family members are needed.

3.2 Measures for quality of life

From a methodological perspective, there is international consensus about the dimensions of quality of life (Schalock et al., 2000). Eight dimensions define the construct of quality of life: emotional wellbeing, interpersonal relationships, material wellbeing, personal development, physical wellbeing, self-determination, social inclusion, and rights (Schalock 2000; Beadle-Brown et al., 2009; Wang et al., 2010). These dimensions have been structured into three main factors: (1) Independence that is composed of personal development and self-determination; (2) Social participation composed of interpersonal relations, social inclusion, and rights; and (3) Wellbeing composed of emotional, physical, and material wellbeing. This model has been empirically validated across different cultures and countries (Schalock & Verdugo, 2005). However, the quality of life literature does not consider these domains as a hierarchy, but rather, these quality of life indicators are considered as quality of life-related perceptions, behaviors, and conditions that operationally define each quality of life domain (Bonham et al., 2004).

A key expression of quality of life is subjective wellbeing that, according to Schalock and Felce (2004), involves two aspects: "satisfaction", representing the global judgments about one's life, and "happiness", reflecting positive and negative effects of positive or negative emotions and moods.

The construct of happiness is difficult to quantify among individuals with nonverbal behavior and low levels of functioning. To overcome this methodological problem, researchers have selected behavioral expressions already connected to possible conditions of pleasure and wellbeing, labeling them as indices of happiness (Lancioni et al., 2005). The indices of happiness are almost overlapping with those signs of positive mood which persons without any disability exhibit in similar situations. Thus, smiling, laughing, and excited body movements with or without vocalizations are considered as indices of happiness.

The literature on indices of happiness in persons with RTT is lacking. Only a recent study (Fabio, Caprì, Nucita, Iannizzotto, & Mohammadhasani, 2019) has tried to quantify the index of happiness through a modified version of the taxonomy of Van der Matt (1992). In this study, the behavior of the girls was recorded. Two independent observers performed a frequency count of the coded behavioral signals for each participant across a time interval. The index of happiness was made by the presence of five out of seven behavioral categories. These behavioral categories included the following behavioral forms: gaze direction, facial expression, sounds, head posture, head movement, body posture, mouth movements, and physiological reactions. The index of happiness, used in this study to evaluate the quality of life in subjects with RTT, seems to be a valid measure in alternatives to hetero-directed methodologies, usually proposed by parents through the interview.

To evaluate the quality of life in subjects with disabilities, including RTT, most frequently used measures are questionnaires or interviews of people that know the person well. Lane and colleagues (2011) used the generic Child Health Questionnaire (Waters et al., 2000) to measure the quality of life of children with RTT. The results obtained indicated that children with more severe impairments had poorer physical quality of life scores, but better psychosocial quality of life scores.

In a recent study, the Caregiver Burden Inventory, designed for Alzheimer's disease, was modified to become the RTT Caregiver Inventory Assessment (RTT CIA). Reliability and face, construct, and concurrent validity were assessed in caregivers of individuals with RTT. Chi square or Fisher's exact test for categorical variables and t tests or Wilcoxon two-sample tests for continuous variables were utilized. Obtained results showed that RTT CIA represented a reliable and valid measure, providing a necessary metric of the caregiver's burden in this disorder.

Epstein and colleagues (2016) explored the quality of life in school-aged children with RTT and compared domains with those identified in other available quality of life scales. Ten domains were identified: physical health, body pain and discomfort, behavioral and emotional wellbeing, communication skills, movement and mobility, social connectedness, variety of activities, provision of targeted services, stability of daily routines, and the natural environment.

Our data articulated important aspects of life beyond the genetic diagnosis. Existing quality of life scales for children in the general population or with other disabilities did not capture the quality of life of children with RTT. Findings support the construction of a new parent-report measure to enable measurement of quality of life in this group.

Overall, the construct of quality of life has been widely evaluated in the field of disability. A systematic search of the disability literature published between 1980 and 2008 was conducted in order to identify and systematically review quality of life measures that could be used by researchers and in measuring subjective and objective quality of life for people who have an intellectual disability. No specific instruments that measure the quality of life of people with ID and challenging behavior were found (Epstein et al., 2016). This finding is very important, because it indicated that instruments used to measure the quality of life in individuals with disabilities are not specific for the syndrome. Moreover, this review underlines that most of the instruments assess quality of life from a subjective perspective, using questionnaire formats and measure only some (not all) of the eight theoretically accepted domains of quality of life, described previously.

In conclusion, more instruments that measure the quality of life of people with disabilities are needed to be built and rigorously validated. Living with the condition of RTT is hard both for the subjects and their families. It is fundamental that all modalities of intervention aimed at improving the quality of life of the girls with RTT must be supported by an action in the living environment of the girls.

3.3 RTT and family system

As seen in the first part of this chapter, RTT affects the family life of the patient, and the family circumstances in turn have an impact upon the individual with RTT. From a medical point of view, the clinical picture of RTT is characterized by stereotypes, oculogyric crises, parkinsonism, dystonia, scoliosis, epilepsy, and respiratory and cardiac diseases. From a psychological perspective, RTT is characterized by intellectual disability, loss of language, attention impairment, and cognitive deficits. This clinical heterogeneous condition requires special care and coordinated multispecialist oriented health care. Consequently, for the family, taking care of a person with RTT is complex, given the multiple needs of these individuals from birth to senescence.

Having a chronic disease, such as RTT, would have an impact on the lives of both patient and other family members. Several authors have described the effects of chronic illness on family functioning according to Family Systems Theory (FST). The FST postulates that family functioning is governed by family structure, and a family's mental health or effectiveness is determined by the degree to which its structures are flexible, resilient, and supportive of change within this network of systems. Family structure is the organized pattern in which family members interact; it doesn't prescribe behavior, but it describes sequences that are predictable. As family transactions are repeated, they foster expectations that establish enduring patterns. Once patterns are established, family members use only a small fraction of the full range of behavior available to them. Moreover, families have some kind of hierarchical structure, with adults and children having different amounts of authority. They are differentiated into subsystems based on generation, gender, and common interests. Family members also tend to have reciprocal and complementary functions (Minuchin, 1974).

Chronic illness can affect this family structure. Sargent (1983) argued that chronic illness may present a crisis for the family, and a family's response to this crisis may be new or more frequent dysfunctional interactions. Salvator Minuchin (1974) was the first author to identify the features of the functioning and adaptation of the family in which a member with chronic disease lives. These were: enmeshment, overprotectiveness, rigidity, and lack of conflict resolution.

Enmeshment is a structural characteristic of the family; it refers to the intensity of boundaries within the family. It is a transactional style, where family members are highly involved with one another. There is excessive togetherness, intrusion on others' thoughts, feelings, and actions, lack of privacy, and weak family boundaries. Members often speak for one another, and perception of the self and other family members is poorly differentiated. A child growing up in this type of family learns that family loyalty is of primary importance. This pattern of interaction hinders separation and individuation later in life.

In other words, enmeshment and disengagement are described as two extreme ends of a continuum: the former is characterized by a lack of boundaries and the latter by very fixed boundaries in the family (Minuchin, 1974). The boundaries refer to invisible barriers that regulate contact with others.

Rigidity is a concept that bears upon the degree of adaptability of the family interaction. It is the pathological pole of the adaptability dimension: it maintains the status quo when external or internal stress causes a need for a change of the usual transactional patterns (Minuchin, 1974). These families are heavily committed to maintaining the status quo. The need for change is denied, thereby preserving accustomed patterns of interaction and behavioral mechanisms.

Overprotectiveness is defined as a high degree of concern for each other's welfare in the family. It refers to the excessive nurturing and protective responses commonly observed. It is also the absence of negotiation in the family. In these families, pacifying behaviors and somatization are prevalent.

Lack of conflict resolution refers to the absence of negotiation in the family. Family members have a low tolerance for overt conflict, and discussions involving differences of opinion are avoided at all costs. Problems are often left unresolved and are prolonged by avoidance maneuvers.

Given the characteristics of RTT, it is reasonable to assume that the family with a member affected by RTT can show the four features described previously. Others factors support this thesis: for instance, persons with RTT generally use more health services than others. The use of these services and related resources are varied and stable for all their lives. This can lead to rigidity within the family structure because the family continually takes care of the patient. In these conditions, in order to maintain positive family interactions, there needs to be less conflict between family members. Moreover, the prevalence of a high degree of positive feelings is an important aspect of family life.

However, high support needs of individual with RTT can lead to personal and financial stress for families and carers. Minuchin (1974) argued that all families are systems in transition, and stress is part of the process of the family adapting and accommodating to new situations. Minuchin (1974) considered stress as a phenomenon flowing from four major sources. Stress from these four sources can originate outside or inside the family system. RTT can be a source of stress for all the reasons discussed in this book.

To our knowledge, few studies have investigated the psychological wellbeing of family members of individuals with RTT. Cianfaglione and colleagues (2015) investigated the psychological wellbeing of mothers and siblings in families of girls and women with RTT. Eightyseven mothers completed the Rett Syndrome Behavior Questionnaire (Mount et al., 2002). This questionnaire is a survey about their daughters' behavioral phenotype, current health, and behavior problems, and their own and a sibling's wellbeing. Results indicated that the mothers showed increased anxiety, but similar levels of depression when compared to a normative sample. Moreover, the severity of their daughters' RTT behavioral phenotype predicted increased anxiety and stress for mothers.

Again, Cianfaglione and colleagues (2016) examined the psychological wellbeing of mothers of girls and women with RTT 16–17 months after an earlier cross-sectional study. The findings confirmed their previous data: more precisely, maternal stress, anxiety, and depression demonstrated at least moderate levels of stability. Maternal positive perceptions were also moderately stable over 16–17 months. The authors claimed that the daughters' behavioral and emotional problems rather than RTT behavioral phenotype severity predicted later maternal wellbeing.

However, not all parents of individuals with RTT report increased levels of psychological distress. For example, Cianfaglione and colleagues (in press) found that 24.1% of mothers of women and girls with RTT reported symptoms of anxiety at levels above a clinical threshold, and 5.7% reported symptoms of depression at elevated levels.

In conclusion, it is very important to recognize the perceptions of the family members and also consider targeted behavioral parent training to reduce behavior problems in individuals with RTT.

3.4 Practical ways to manage the condition in the family

Most individuals with RTT require maximum assistance with every aspect of daily living. The basics of caregiving include what the parents or the caregivers do every day: feed, bathe, clothe, toilet, and possibly give medication. Caregivers may have to lift and carry them, or help them walk, reposition them often for comfort, or change a bib for drool. They might have to program and reprogram a communication device. They must know how to operate with eye-trackers or other tools and keep a DVD or MP3 player charged at all times. They have to learn how to find the right professionals, schedule appointments and therapies, search for the right schools or programs, and provide special equipment. Thus, it is reasonable to claim that living with RTT can be very hard for caregivers and families.

A practical way to manage family conditions is to improve the communicative abilities of the girls with RTT. As seen in this book, the lack of language in subjects with RTT creates severe difficulties for the caregivers in understanding the individual's needs and wishes. Not only is this difficult for the families, but also for the patient itself. Sigafoos and colleagues (2000, 2006) noted that caregivers often report that their child uses various informal and idiosyncratic behaviors (e.g. vocalizations, body movements, facial expressions) to communicate. For instance, a subject with RTT who consistently looks at an object for several seconds when it is first brought within view; if caregivers interpret the subject's eye gaze response as a communicative act, equivalent to a spoken request (e.g. "I want that object"), then they might be inclined to give the person whatever he/she happens to look at. These behaviors can be interpreted as a communicative signal, but it is also plausible that the child's eye gaze was merely a simple orienting or reflexive response. A review (Sigafoos et al., 2010) examined the studies aimed at determining whether behaviors, such as body movements, vocalizations, eye gaze, and facial expressions, served a communicative function for individuals with RTT. The results indicated that participants showed behaviors serving as communicative functions, including eye pointing/eye gaze, body movements, leading, clapping, reaching, pushing away items, tantrums/screaming.

In this scenario, it is very important to improve the communicative conditions between family members and patients. Sigafoos and colleagues (2006) suggest a three-step approach to achieve this purpose:

1. To conduct structured caregiver interviews in order to identify and objectively describe any existing behaviors that caregivers perceive to be forms of communication;
2. To use standardized tests in order to validate the information from the interviews;
3. To design and implement structured behavioral observations in order to determine if any of the identified behaviors from steps 1 and 2 are differentially sensitive to various types of communication opportunities (e.g. opportunities for requesting, rejecting, and greeting).

Subsequently, this information could be used to develop a specific intervention in order to focus on strengthening existing communicative forms or replacing existing forms with more advanced and formal communicative responses (Sigafoos et al., 2006).

Most training to develop communication abilities in persons with RTT consist of Augmentative and Alternative Communication (AAC) programs and cognitive empowerment combined with eye-tracking technology (see Chapter 4). These interventions aim to improve the person's ability to express wants and needs, initiate conversations, and more generally participate in communicative exchanges with others (Reichle et al., 1991).

AAC is the term used to describe various methods that can be used to help people with disabilities communicate with others. AAC includes simple systems such as pictures, gestures, and pointing, as well as more complex techniques involving powerful computer technology. Examples of AAC methods including gestures, facial expressions, vocalizations, and pictures are the following:

- Using an actual object to convey meaning; for example, your child hands you a cup to let you know she is thirsty;
- Pointing to symbols, such as pictures or textures on a communication board or in a book;
- Activating a device; for example, your child presses a switch or button on a recorded speech device, initiating auditory output that says "I'm thirsty".

There is a wide array of ACC devices. For example, a communication board can be made out of cardboard, wood, or another solid surface. Typically it has a grid on it with two or more symbols. The symbols can be concrete, such as actual objects or parts of objects; pictorial, such as photographs or drawings; alphabet symbols in print or braille; or words in print or braille. Another example is a communication book in which a subject with speech disabilities can point to specific symbols in order to convey her message. The symbols have broad categories, such as emotions, foods, and people.

Electronic systems are often the first choice, as they can offer the added bonus of speech output and convey a positive image. Low-tech paper and chart-based systems are easier to set up and manage, though it must be stressed that choosing an appropriate vocabulary for any system and method is not a trivial task. The lack of speech output can be a big restriction for some users whose peers may be unable to understand a printed system (for more details, please see Chapter 5).

A large body of literature focusing on communicative training in RTT (Fabio et al., 2009; Sigafoos et al., 2009; Sigafoos, Kagohara, et al., 2011; Sigafoos, Wermink, et al., 2011) has shown that the girls improve their communicative forms (e.g. body movement, eye gaze, or vocalizations) to gain attention and to answer others. Consequently, the improvement of communicative abilities represents an important factor to improve the family condition, because the parents have the possibility to give meaning to the behaviors emitted by the girls.

A review (Sigafoos et al., 2011) on communicative abilities in the girls with RTT has also indicated that these girls use a range of behaviors to communicate, including eye pointing/eye gaze, body movements, leading, clapping, reaching, pushing away items, and tantrums/screaming. Moreover, such behaviors include the use of stereotyped hand movements, facial expressions, body movements, (undifferentiated) vocalizations, eye gaze, and even hyperventilation, and are commonly acknowledged to be in order to seek attention, protest, request, or make a choice (Townend et al., 2016). Based on this behavioral repertoire, it is important for operators, doctors, psychologists, and educators to empower and pay attention to the communicative capacities of the girls in order to improve the living environment of the girls.

In accordance with these suggestions, several studies have shown that the AAC intervention (Beukelman & Mirenda, 2005; Schlosser, 2003) is a useful tool for girls with RTT in order to improve the person's ability to express wants and needs, initiate conversations, and more generally participate in communicative exchanges with others.

As seen in Chapter 2, the aim of AAC is to provide an individual with a means of independent communication and to maximize their ability and opportunity to successfully participate in everyday environments. Therefore, it is very important for parents to learn the technique of AAC to communicate with daughter. In particular, parents should learn the methodology for the intention of understanding, such as to say "yes" and "no". This is a fundamental condition for understanding the needs of girls with RTT. If you are interested in the methodology for a communication intervention, please see Chapter 5.

3.5 Conclusion

In conclusion, a well-functioning intervention program must also include appropriate involvement and collaboration with the individual's family. Intervention should be focused and individualized and must be broadly implemented to relate to the full range of impairments shown by the client. Regardless of the individual's age, treatment planning should include provision for structured opportunities for learning and for generalization of what is learned (Lotan, 2006). The potential outcome for these girls and their families is to achieve some functional skills and maintain them. Overall, this chapter has illustrated a number of practical ways in which parents might attempt to manage the family environment in which the girls with RTT live.

Caring for a child with RTT is both a practical and an emotional burden for parents. A subject with RTT, in addition to the care requirements during the school years, needs care and emotional support and the availability of an attachment figure for a long time. Burdens of basic care are high, and families who care for a child with RTT perform meaningful societal services which are expected, but not adequately valued and offered by society (Schalock, 2000). In order to support families with a member with RTT, international Rett Syndrome support networks have been created by groups of parents or associations. In the last chapter, Chapter 6, we discuss the most common RTT international associations in the world that can help to find more information on legislation, rights, and interventions in each country.

References

Beadle-Brown, J., Murphy, G. & diTerlizzi, M. (2009). Quality of life for the Camberwell Cohort. *Journal of Applied Research in Intellectual Disabilities*, 22, 380–390.

Bonham, G.S., Basehart, S., Schalock, R.L., Marchand, C.B., Kirchner, N. & Rumenap, J.M. (2004). Consumer based quality of life assessment: the Maryland Ask Me Project. *Mental Retardation*, 42(5), 338–355.

Cianfaglione, R., Hastings, R.P., Felce, D., Clarke, A. & Kerr, M.P. (2017). Change over a 16-month period in the psychological well-being of mothers of girls and women with Rett syndrome. *Journal Developmental Neurorehabilitation*, 20, 261–265.

Esposito, M. et al. (2013). Executive dysfunction in children affected by obstructive sleep apnea syndrome: an observational study. *Neuropsychiatric Disease and Treatment*, 9, 1087–1094.

Epstein, A. et al. (2016). Conceptualizing a quality of life framework for girls with Rett syndrome using qualitative methods. *American Journal of Medicine and Genetics*, 170(3), 645–653.

Fabio, R.A., Caprì, T., Nucita, A., Iannizzotto, G. & Mohammadhasani, N. (2019). The role of eye gaze digital games to improve motivational and attentional ability in Rett syndrome. *Journal of Special Education and Rehabilitation*, 9(3–4), 105–126.

Hetzroni, O. & Rubin, C. (2006). Identifying patterns of communicative behaviors in girls with Rett syndrome. *Augmentative and Alternative Communication*, 22, 48–61.

Killian, J.T. et al. (2016). Caretaker quality of life in Rett syndrome: disorder features and psychological predictors. *Pediatric Neurology*, 58, 67–74.

Lancioni, G.E., Singh, N.N., O'Reilly, M.F., Oliva, D. & Basili, G. (2005). An overview of research on increasing indices of happiness of people with severe/profound intellectual and multiple disabilities. *Journal Disability and Rehabilitation*, 25(3), 83–93.

Lane, J.B. et al. (2011). Clinical severity and quality of life in children and adolescents with Rett Syndrome. *Neurology*, 77, 1812–1818.

Laurvick, C.L., De Klerk, N., Bower, C., Christodoulou, J., Ravine, D., Ellaway, C. & Leonard, H. (2006). Rett syndrome in Australia: a review of the epidemiology. *The Journal of Pediatrics*, 148(3), 347–352.

Matson, J.L., Dempsey, T. & Wilkins, J. (2008). Rett syndrome in adults with severe intellectual disability: exploraration of behavioural characteristics. *European Psychiatry*, 23, 460–465.

Minuchin, S. (1974). *Families and Family Therapy*. Cambridge, MA: Harvard University Press.

Naidu, S. et al. (2003). Variability in the Rett syndrome. *Journal of Child Neurology*, 18, 662–668.

Parisi, L., Di Filippo, T. & Roccella, M. (2016). The quality of life in girls with Rett syndrome. *Mental illness*, 8(1), 6302.

Sarajlija, A., Djuric, M. & Tepavcevic, D.K. (2013). Health-related quality of life and depression in Rett syndrome caregivers. *Vojnosanit Pregl*, 70, 842–847.

Schalock, R.L. (2000). Three decades of quality of life. In *Mental Retardation in the 21st Century*, eds M.L. Wehmeyer & J.R. Patton, 335–356. Austin, TX: Pro-ed.

Schalock, R.L., Brown, I., Brown, R., Cummins, R.A., Felce, D., Matikka, L., Keith, K.D. & Parmenter, T. (2002). Conceptualization, measurement, and application of quality of life for people with intellectual disabilities: report of an international panel of experts. *Mental Retardation*, 40(6), 457–470.

Schalock, R.L. & Felce, D. (2004). Quality of life and subjective well-being: conceptual and measurement issues. In *International Handbook on Methods for Research and Evaluation in Intellectual Disabilities*, eds E. Emerson, T. Thompson, T. Parmenter & C. Hatton, 261–280. New York: Wiley.

Schalock, R.L. & Verdugo, M.A. (2005). Cross-cultural study of quality of life indicators. *American Journal on Mental Retardation*, 110, 298–311.

Sigafoos, J., Woodyatt, G., Keen, D., Tait, K., Tucker, M., Roberts-Pennell, D. & Pittendreigh, N. (2000). Identifying potential communicative acts in children with developmental and physical disabilities. *Communication Disorders Quarterly*, 21(2), 77–86.

Stasolla, F. & Caffò, A.O. (2013). Promoting adaptive behaviors by two girls with Rett syndrome through a microswitch-based program. *Research in Autism Spectrum Disorders*, 7, 1265–1272.

Temudo, T., Freitas, P., Sequeiros, G., Maciel, P. & Oliveira, G. (2008). Atypical stereotypies and vocal tics in Rett Syndrome: an illustrative case. *Movement Disorder*, 23(4), 622–624.

Van der Maat, S. (1992). *Communicatie tussen personen met een diep mentale handicap enhun opvoed(st)ers [Communication between persons with a profound intellectual disability and their primary caregivers]*. Leuven, Belgium: Garant.

Waters, E., Salmon, L., Wake, M., Hesketh, K. & Wright, M. (2000). The Child Health Questionnaire in Australia: reliability, validity and population means. *Australian and New Zealand Journal of Public Health*, 24, 207–210.

Chapter 4

Treatment and therapy

The aim of the present chapter is to describe in depth the latest psycho-educational approaches to Rett Syndrome (RTT). Overall, the psycho-educational model is a humanistic approach to changing behavior patterns, values, interpretation of events, and life outlook of individuals who are not adjusting well to their environment (e.g. home, school). Appropriate behaviors are developed by helping people to display better behavior choices. Psycho-education is not a treatment; in clinical settings, psychoeducation is the first step of the overall treatment plan. Current psycho-educational approaches have emerged from blending developmental, cognitive, and learning psychological theories.

This chapter begins with a theoretical overview of multidisciplinary treatments for RTT and then focuses on specific cognitive and communication training. Early interventions can significantly improve the health and quality of life of individuals with RTT. In the first part of this chapter, we will discuss the rehabilitation programs which are appropriate for patients' needs, the importance of control of movement, and interaction in communication. In the second part, new therapeutic approaches will be discussed, such as the use of eye-tracker technologies, virtual reality programs, and cognitive empowerment. Moreover, intervention with transcranial direct current stimulation (tDCS) and pharmacological treatment will be analyzed along with an in-depth description of the methodological procedures. As we saw in the previous chapters, Rett Syndrome is a complex disorder and the wide variety of symptoms described in Chapter 1 and Chapter 2 alter the quality of life of the persons with RTT, as seen in Chapter 3. The premise of the present book is that modifiability is possible and that with the correct treatments, persons with Rett Syndrome can reach more comfortable and enjoyable lives. As a second premise, it's important that educators and therapists are using research-validated interventions and approaches to treat and improve the symptoms associated with Rett Syndrome. Research is providing continuous

Figure 4.1 Traditional treatments for RTT.

up-to-date training and the aim of the present chapter is to describe both the traditional and the latest approaches to RTT.

Due to the complexity of the symptoms, the treatments are complex too. For each group of symptoms of RTT disease, there are specific treatments (see Figure 4.1). Here following, we will discuss some treatments related to each of the following areas.

4.1 Traditional treatments

Physical therapy, also known as physiotherapy, is the use of mechanical force and movements (bio-mechanics or kinesiology), manual therapy, exercise therapy, and electrotherapy to remediate impairments and promote mobility and function. It is also used to improve a patient's quality of life through examination, diagnosis, prognosis, and physical intervention. The specific aims with girls with Rett syndrome are to improve or maintain mobility and balance, to reduce misshapen back and limbs, and to provide weight-bearing training for patients with scoliosis. PT is also directed toward preventing deformities, such as reducing joint contractures. Weight-bearing exercises are helpful for bone health. Maintaining good postural alignment and bracing may help to slow the progression of scoliosis. Physical assistance, braces, or surgery are used to correct scoliosis, and splints to adjust hand movements; for a review, see the studies of Lotan and Hanks (2006). Lotan and Hanks have written a review on common intervention approaches for individuals with RTT and their present day's application. Based on his clinical experience, the author suggests some guidelines for motor individual intervention with patients with RTT. Specifically, Lotan and Hanks (2006) suggest:

1. Before the beginning of any intervention, the physical therapist should familiarize the child with each therapeutic session;

2. During therapy sessions, it is advisable to allow the child to gain control over the sessions by enabling her to choose her preferred activity via an appropriate communication device, such as the eye-tracker;

3. The intensity of activities should be adjusted according to the reaction of the child. For example, if the child is having a difficult time adjusting to physical activity, the speed of the intervention should be adjusted using motivational factors, such as music, switch-operated games, videotapes, pets, and/or family members.

Occupational therapy is the use of assessment and intervention to develop, recover, or maintain the meaningful activities, or occupations, of individuals, groups, or communities. With Rett Syndrome, occupational therapy is useful because it improves or maintains the use of hands, reduces stereotypic hand movements such as wringing, washing (a movement that resembles washing the hands), clapping, rubbing, or tapping and teaches self-directed activities like dressing and feeding. Here, we offer some examples of goals: identify and encourage use of head, elbows, or other body parts over which she may have better control; maximise hand use for functional activities; develop ability to access communication devices; develop ability to access a variety of assistive technology; improve ability to assist with dressing; improve ability to perform independent feeding skills; improve ability to assist with grooming activities.

Speech-language therapy provides treatment, support, and care for children and adults who have difficulties with communication, or with eating, drinking, and swallowing. In RTT, it is useful to teach nonverbal communication and improve social interaction. Speech and language therapy will focus on improving, supporting, and developing the communication skills of individuals with Rett Syndrome. Speech and language therapy will usually work on receptive (understanding) and expressive communication through the use of Alternative and Augmentative Communication (AAC). AAC is any form of communication other than speech. Types of AAC used for individuals with Rett Syndrome may include:

- Picture symbols;
- Objects of reference;
- Sign language;
- Learning of reading abilities.

Use of AAC helps to develop receptive communication and reduce frustration by allowing the individual with Rett Syndrome to express their wants and needs. AAC can consist of hi-tech communication aids e.g. use of computer software and electronic communication systems. AAC also includes low-tech aids which generally consist of pictures, symbols, objects of reference, and use of the individual's body to communicate. In the next chapter, we will better specify the use of AAC techniques in school. Family members, caregivers, and school staff should be trained on how best to support the use of AAC for subjects with RTT. Training should be done by a clinician who is knowledgeable in AAC. The aim of parent training should be to: show you how to use AAC with your child; help you choose appropriate vocabulary for your child; teach you to program and operate your child's communication device.

Feeding assistance is the action of a person feeding another person who could not otherwise feed themselves. The term is used in the context of some medical issue or in response to a disability, such as when a person living with dementia is no longer able to manage eating alone. Nutritional and caloric intake must be monitored. Nutritional supplements may be prescribed if caloric intake is not adequate. If the child breathes in (aspirates) food or has difficulty chewing, then a feeding tube may be helpful. Liquid nutrients can be delivered directly to the stomach via the tube inserted through the nose (short term) or through the abdominal wall (longer term). Getting necessary nutrients and maintaining an adequate weight may result in enhanced attentiveness, improved social interactions, and optimal growth, and provide an adequate intake of fluids and high-fiber foods to avoid or relieve constipation. Maintaining an intake of recommended daily allowances of calcium and vitamins is important for health. In particular, bone health is important in girls with Rett Syndrome, given the prevalence of osteoporosis.

Assisted feeding happens when a caretaker puts food into the mouth of the person who has difficulty eating. This is useful in circumstances when the person needing assistance can swallow the food, but only fails to bring the food to their mouth. Supplements such as calcium and minerals are used to strengthen bones and slow scoliosis; a high-calorie, high-fat diet is followed to increase height and weight; insertion of a feeding tube will assist if patients accidentally swallow their food into their lungs.

The interventions of **medication** are multiple: to reduce breathing problems; to eliminate problems with abnormal heart rhythm; to relieve indigestion and constipation; to control seizures. With reference to seizures, if seizures are suspected, an EEG may be obtained as well as a referral to a neurologist. Medications are prescribed to control seizure activity for many girls affected by Rett Syndrome. Input from a neurologist is important since some children with Rett Syndrome have seizures that are refractory to treatment. Also, some of the breathing abnormalities seen in Rett Syndrome may be confused with seizure events.

- Muscle stiffness, breathing irregularities (while awake), heart arrhythmias, constipation, gastrointestinal reflux ("heart burn"), anxiety, difficulties with sleeping, and severe agitation may occur in some children with Rett Syndrome. If a child has these symptoms, they should be evaluated and may be treated with medication.
- Orthopedic management is important for optimizing gait/ skeletal alignment and for management of contractures and scoliosis.
- Cardiac: sudden death has been reported to occur more commonly in individuals with Rett Syndrome than the general population. It is not completely clear what causes this. However, many individuals with Rett Syndrome have been found to have an abnormality on their electrocardiogram called prolonged QT. It is important for individuals with Rett Syndrome to be evaluated for abnormality on electrocardiogram and to avoid medications which are known to prolong the QT. The International Rett Syndrome Association (IRSA) recommends the first electrocardiogram (EKG) should be performed by age five and, if normal, repeated every other year. Hearing and vision should be evaluated and monitored regularly.

Gene therapy. RTT was shown to be fully reversible in a mouse model of the disease, indicating that it could be amenable to gene therapy. This is of primary importance, as most RTT mutations occur de novo, and the disease is usually diagnosed when the symptoms are present, which also means that any therapeutic intervention will be administered to RTT patients after disease onset. The academic community is aware that gene therapy and gene editing are still in their infancy, but this idea is not such common knowledge among the families of those affected. There is not enough information available to lay persons to allow realistic expectations to be set for the "cure"

(Clarke & Sheikh, 2018). We should be careful in interpreting the results in the genetic research field.

Alternative approaches. Other health care professionals are vital members of the health care team involved in the treatment of people with Rett Syndrome. They include: orthopedic surgeons, gastroenterologists, pulmonologists, cardiologists, neurologists, developmental specialists, developmental pediatricians, special education providers, and nurses.

Alternative approaches such as hydrotherapy (therapy using water to strengthen muscles and help alleviate pain), massage therapy, and hippotherapy (a treatment strategy that utilizes a horse's movement to provide sensory input).

Hydrotherapy is an exercise program carried out in a therapy pool. It can be used to decrease discomfort and increase range of motion. The effects appear to last for a few weeks after each session. Horseback riding has also been used to increase balance as well as the emotional wellbeing of the children, but its results have not been scientifically reported.

There are two types of hydrotherapy:

1. Therapeutic swimming uses simple movements in water to find confidence in one's body, to lower anxiety, and to increase self-confidence. A physiotherapist/aquatic therapist conducts it (see Figure 4.2).

Figure 4.2 Example of therapeutic swimming.

2. "Water cure" or "bath therapy" is part of alternative medicine that uses water buoyancy to relieve physical pain. A physiotherapist conducts it (see Figure 4.3).

Parents can help the physiotherapist assessing the needs and abilities of their child with RTT and devise a program appropriate to her requirements. As a parent, you know best what your daughter can and can't do, what skills she has had and lost, what movements she likes, and those she avoids. You will also be aware of her limitations. You also will have some ideas of what you want for your child. With the physiotherapist, you can devise reasonable and achievable goals for daily life.

Music therapy is also often a common intervention used in RTT. It can encourage functional hand use through manipulation of the instruments, as well as interaction through the alertness created by the music. It may also facilitate communication and is simply just an enjoyable activity for the child. We suggest some guidance actions for parents who want to use music therapy, as follows:

1. First, use a sound favored by your child. Second, play eye-catching instruments, such as an ocean drum or radiant tambourine in different positions to help visual tracking.

Figure 4.3 Example of water cure.

2. Use pictures of favorite songs, instruments, or singers during choice-making activities.
3. Add musical instrument sound effects to stories to gain attention and focus.

Each of these treatments have been studied in detail. We cannot deal with each of these treatments exhaustively, so if you are interested, it is better to consult specific books.

4.2 Common principles of treatments

A common ground of all the interventions is the principles related to the empowerment of each area. The term "empowerment" has a considerable intuitive appeal; however, it is difficult to define and it embraces numerous ambiguities. For example, it refers to both a process and an outcome. Empowerment is the process by which individuals, groups, and/or communities are able take control of their circumstances and achieve goals, thereby being able to work towards maximizing the quality of a common denominator of intellectually disabled children. There are two major standpoints. The basic principles which inspire the intervention are modifiability and mediated learning. Modifiability refers to the capacity of human beings to change or modify the structure of their cognitive functioning (thinking skills) to adapt to changing demands in life situations. Modifiability is not a biological or maturational change; it occurs in specific conditions: when (1) change in a part affects the whole to which the changed part belongs; (2) when the process of the change is transformed in its rhythm, amplitude, and direction; and (3) when the change is self-perpetuating, reflecting its autonomous, self-regulatory nature. For example, an individual with a stroke can recover his memory skills if specifically trained. According to Feuerstein and colleagues (1988), modifiability can be applied despite the presence of severe impairments in individuals and/or the harsh difficulties in their environment, which is the case in subjects with RTT. For these reasons, we think that learning and empowerment of specific skills (cognitive, motor, or communication) are also possible in people with RTT. However, to assist in learning, it is not sufficient to expose them to a rich world of colors, objects of different forms, sounds, and movements without changing their relationship with these stimuli so that their experience does not remain superficial. In other words, the capacity for change is related to the mediated learning experience.

This term refers to learning that occurs when another human (caregiver, parent, teacher, peer) interposes him or herself between the stimuli (or the learner's response) and the learner, with the intention of mediating the stimuli or response to the learner. For example, a parent can teach a child with RTT about relevant objects (food, animals, toys) and indicate which objects are dangerous or not, explain their meaning, and create for his or her child a direct experience with such objects, and develop cognitive prerequisites for such direct learning. This mediated learning experience helps the child with RTT to develop a disposition to attend to the stimuli to which she is being directly exposed.

4.2.1 The psychological bases of empowerment

Most educational interventions with intellectually disabled students have set poor goals (e.g. simply dealing with information); such a small investment prevents the development of the ability of "learning to learn". What is important, in fact, is not that the subject becomes able to reproduce information, but that he/she can gradually modify his/her underlying cognitive processes. Cognitive empowerment has the theoretical basis on the Vygotsky's zone of proximal development theory and on Feurstein's modifiability theory. The zone of proximal development, known as ZPD, is the difference between what a learner can do without help and what he or she can do with help (see Figure 4.4).

Vygotsky stated that a child follows an adult's example and gradually develops the ability to do certain tasks without help or assistance. Vygotsky's often-quoted definition of the zone of proximal development presents it as the distance between the actual developmental level as determined by independent problem-solving and the level

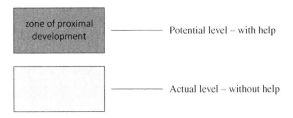

Figure 4.4 The Vygotsky zone of proximal development.

of potential development as determined through problem-solving under adult guidance, or in collaboration with a more capable peer. Vygotsky among other educational professionals believes the role of education is to provide children with experiences which are in their ZPD, thereby encouraging and advancing their individual learning. The lower limit of ZPD is the level of skill reached by the child working independently. The upper limit is the level of additional responsibility the child can accept with the assistance of an able instructor. The ZPD captures the child's cognitive skills that are in the process of maturing and can be accomplished only with the assistance of a more skilled person.

Scaffolding is a concept closely related to the idea of ZPD. Scaffolding involves changing the level of support. Scaffolding is a process through which a teacher or a more competent peer gives aid to the student in her/his ZPD as necessary, and tapers off this aid as it becomes unnecessary, much as a scaffold is removed from a building during construction. Over the course of a teaching session, a more skilled person adjusts the amount of guidance to fit the child's current performance (see Figure 4.5 and Figure 4.6).

This concept has been further developed by Ann Brown, among others. Ann Brown was an educational psychologist who argued that children's learning difficulties often stem from an inability to use metacognitive strategies. Her work is still relevant because she developed methods for teaching children to be better learners. Several instructional programs were developed on the basis of the notion of ZPD and Brown's work, including reciprocal teaching and dynamic assessment (Castelli et al., 2013; Fabio, Antonietti, Castelli, & Marchetti, 2009; Fabio et al., 2016; Fabio, Castelli, Marchetti, & Antonietti, 2013; Fabio, Giannatiempo, Antonietti, & Budden, 2009).

Figure 4.5 The scaffolding process: adult's hands help child's hands, adult's hands start to decrease the level of help, and adult's hands leave child's hands.

Vygotsky's ZPD can be expanded to the examination of other domains of competence and skills. These specialized zones of development include cultural zones, individual zones, and skill-oriented zones. Of these skill-oriented zones, it is commonly believed among early childhood development researchers that young children learn their native language and motor skills in general by being placed in the zone of proximal development.

In the Feuerstein view, to help these students learn, it is not enough to expose them to a rich world of colours, objects of different forms, sounds, and movements, without changing their relationship with these stimuli so that they do not remain superficial. In order to change an experience into a source of learning, some components are necessary. These components induce the individual to classify, make comparisons, group, label, and convey meaning to his current experience, putting it in relation to previous ones.

This active way of experiencing the world is the result of a form of interaction, the so-called "experience of mediated learning". Mediation means that a change can be caused by another human person (H) that puts him/herself with an active behavior and with precise intentions between the other person (O) and a stimulus (S); therefore, he/she has the role of a mediator. Thanks to an experience of mediated learning, the organism (O) that is directly exposed to the stimuli (S) receives them and answers them with adequate competences only after their features have been selected, framed, and modified by an adult human mediator (H). All the individual learning is organized by the adult mediator who determines the relations among stimuli. In other words, in educational and rehabilitative relationships, the educator should select some stimuli, set them into a time sequence (before and after) and according to purpose, put them into a causal and spatial system, attach a special meaning to certain stimuli, propose them many times, cancel other ones, highlight associations among some stimuli, and avoid other ones.

In the Feuerstein view, parents can be active-modifying mediators that shape a child's development. Mediator's behavior can be expressed verbally: for example, "Wow, very good" if your daughter looks at objects to express her need (a bottle of water). It can be also expressed nonverbally by facial expression, tone of voice, and repetitious actions that convey the significance of the object or event: for example, you can look or smile when your daughter looks at an object or spontaneously produces a sound (vocal or consonant).

Finally, it is important that this kind of intervention takes place at three levels: cognitive, emotional, and behavioral. In effect, the

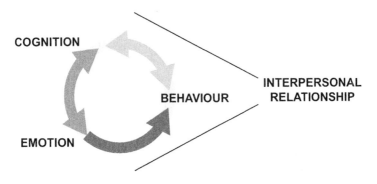

Figure 4.6 Levels of intervention.

basis underlying this methodology is the human relationship (see Figure 4.6).

The relationship is intended both as an instrument of mediation to improve the student with RTT's abilities and as a way to restore a meaning to the world itself through the interaction with the adult. At the cognitive level, children with RTT have learned the basic discriminations that are necessary to understand reality: they have learned to recognize common objects, images of common objects, colors, shapes, and dimensions. For example, you can teach your daughter to look at food if she needs to eat. At an emotional level, she has learned to recognize basic emotions and complex ones on her mother's face and then to generalize them on other significant partners' faces (father, teacher, educator). You can teach her to recognize partners' faces using their pictures and nominating them for each exposure. At the behavior level, you can teach her to touch a relevant object to express her need.

4.2.2 The biological bases of cognitive empowerment

The biological bases of cognitive empowerment normally refer to the concept of "neuroplasticity" (also referred to as brain plasticity, cortical plasticity, or cortical re-mapping).

Neuroplasticity is the ability of the brain that allows us to learn and adapt to our environment. Many studies have shown that plasticity is retained throughout the lifespan from infancy to old age. The results of these studies suggest that the training can improve neural plasticity and functional recovery after a lesion. Rehabilitative therapy, indeed, avoids a further loss of the representation of the physical structure within the intact cortex and induces an expansion of the area in the adjacent cortex. Even though during the last decades, a lot of scientists have revealed the possibility of recovering cortical functions after a lesion, which confirms that the human brain is physiologically sensitive in respect of the experience, and its plasticity is maintained in the case of a lesion. The ability to learn new motor-cognitive skills, with an intact CNS, is similar to the recovery of abilities after damage. Therefore, the brain has the possibility to compensate for cerebral lesions with specific mechanisms. This phenomenon consists of two processes: the functional reorganization of neuronal circuits, and their structural reconstruction. In the case of functional reorganization, the recovery depends on the entirety of the structures that perform functions that normally are not relevant to them, without the need to stop the activities that they were performing until then. Instead, according to the concept of redundancy, our brain has many more neurons that it actually uses, so if a part is damaged, another can replace their functions (see Figure 4.7).

To recover their functions, neurons have to connect to each other. When neurons connect to one another, they require energy and matter to build dendrites.

Using positron emission tomography, an interesting result is that in a person who learns to solve a particular problem effectively, when asked to do the problem over again, the blood flow is much less intense. Indeed, as we know, when a problem has been solved repeatedly, we solve it without effort. We interpret these results to indicate that once structures have been formed, much material and energy are no longer required; the process of learning stops. What has been learned is strengthened by repetition (Fabio et al., 2009; Fabio et al., 2018; Fabio et al., 2018; Fabio et al., 2018; Gangemi et al., 2018; Vignoli et al., 2010).

Increasing proper connections among the brain's neurons results in a better functioning brain. These connections result, in part, through inherited growth patterns within the genetic makeup of a person. They also develop in response to stimuli in the environment that the brain encodes as nerve impulses. The implication here for educators is obvious. Since brains increase dendritic growth as a result of enriching experiences, and since growth is stabilized by practice and rehearsal, the school environment can and should provide such experiences. Doing so will help students retain what they have learned and increase the likelihood of their being able to apply that learning to new situations.

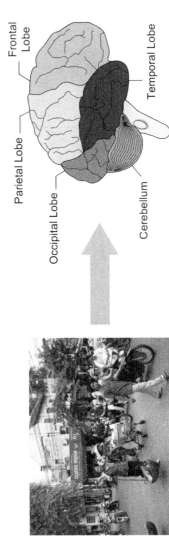

Figure 4.7 The environment changes the brain.

Before starting and showing the basic principles of empowerment and enrichment, it is important to verify the assessment of the abilities of girls with Rett Syndrome.

4.3 Conclusion

Most people with RTT benefit from well-designed interventions no matter what their age, but the earlier that treatment begins, the better. With therapy and assistance, people with Rett Syndrome can participate in school and community activities. These treatments, forms of assistance, and options for medication generally aim to slow the loss of abilities, improve or preserve movement, and encourage communication and social contact. There are a number of ways to help reduce the effects of RTT.

Most treatments are supportive and aim at addressing specific symptoms of Rett Syndrome rather than trying to take on the disorder as an entire entity. Generally speaking, the goal of these treatments is to hold back the decline in abilities, enhance or maintain movement, and support social contact and communication. Most families and physicians find that what works best is a complex, interdisciplinary approach that includes many diverse kinds of therapies. These therapies, which range from traditional approaches to new and experimental ones, may include other health care professionals who are vital members of the healthcare team involved in the treatment of people with Rett Syndrome. They include: orthopedic surgeons, gastroenterologists, pulmonologists, cardiologists, neurologists, developmental specialists, developmental pediatricians, psychologists, special education providers, and nurses.

A number of promising interventions targeted towards promoting neuroplasticity have been identified. The new technologies that facilitate synaptogenesis processes in patients with brain injury or neurodegenerative diseases have evolved. Several forms of non-invasive brain stimulation have been examined as potentially changing brain function and thereby promoting neuroplasticity. These new interventions for RTT will described in the next chapter.

References

Castelli, I., Antonietti, A., Fabio, R.A., Lucchini, B. & Marchetti, A. (2013). Do Rett syndrome persons possess Theory of Mind? Some evidence from non-treated girls. *Life Span and Disability*, XVI(2), 157–168.

Fabio, R.A., Antonietti, A., Marchetti, A. & Castelli, I. (2009). Attention and communication in Rett syndrome. *Research in Autism Spectrum Disorders*, 3, 329–335.

Fabio, R.A., Billeci, L., Crifaci, G., Troise, E., Tortorella, G. & Pioggia, G. (2016). Cognitive training modifies frequency EEG bands and neuropsychological measures in Rett syndrome. *Research in Developmental Disabilities*, *54*, 73–85.

Fabio, R.A., Caprì, T., Lotan, M., Towey, G.E. & Martino, G. (2018). Motor abilities are related to the specific genotype in Rett syndrome. In *Advances in Genetic Research*, vol. 18, chapter id 32719, 79–108. New York: Nova Science Publisher.

Fabio, R.A., Castelli, I., Marchetti, A. & Antonietti, A. (2013). Training communication abilities in Rett syndrome through reading and writing. *Frontiers in Psychology*, *911*, 1–9.

Fabio, R.A., Colombo, B., Russo, S., Cogliati, S.F., Masciandri, M., Antonietti, A. & Tavian, D. (2014). Recent Insights into genotype-phenotype relationships in patients with Rett Syndrome using a fine grain scale. *Research in Developmental Disabilities*, *35*(11), 2976–2986.

Fabio, R.A., Gangemi, A., Capri, T., Budden, S. & Falzone, A. (2018). Neurophysiological and cognitive effects of Transcranial Direct Current Stimulation in three girls with Rett Syndrome with chronic language impairments. *Research in Developmental Disabilities*, *76*, 76–87.

Fabio, R.A., Giannatiempo, S., Antonietti, A. & Budden, S. (2009). The role of stereotypies in overselectivity processes in Rett syndrome. *Research in Developmental Disabilities*, *30*, 136–145.

Fabio, R.A., Giannatiempo, S., Oliva, P. & Murdaca, A.M. (2011). The increase of attention in Rett Syndrome. A pretest-post test research design. *Journal of Developmental and Physical Disability*, *23*, 99–111.

Fabio, R.A., Magaudda, C., Caprì, T., Towey, G. & Martino, G. (2018). Choice behavior in Rett syndrome, the consistency parameter. *Life Span and Disability*, *XXXI*(1), 47–62.

Gangemi, A., Caprì, T., Fabio, R.A., Puggioni, P., Falzone, A. & Martino, G. (2018). Transcranial Direct Current Stimulation (tDCS) and Cognitive Empowerment for the functional recovery of diseases with chronic impairment and genetic etiopathogenesis. In *Advances in Genetic Research*, vol. 18, 179–196. New York: Nova Science Publisher.

Lotan, M. & Susan, H. (2006). Physical therapy intervention for individuals with Rett syndrome. *The Scientific World Journal*, *6*, 1314–1338.

Vignoli, A., Fabio, R.A., La Briola, F., Giannatiempo, S., Antonietti, A, Maggiolini, S. & Canevini, M.P. (2010). Correlations between neurophysiological, behavioral, and cognitive function in Rett syndrome. *Epilepsy & Behavior*, *17*, 489–496.

Chapter 5

From assessment to intervention

Each intervention starts with an assessment of the person's abilities. An educational assessment has to be conducted to determine the individual needs of each person affected with Rett Syndrome (RTT) because there is a wide potential range of abilities.

5.1 The assessment of abilities

To assess the abilities of intellectually disabled children, we can use both functional scales and task analysis procedures. Here, we present two groups of functional scales: the Vineland Adaptive Behavior Scales (VABS) and the Rett Assessment Rating Scale (RARS). The VABS is the most commonly used functional scale to measure adaptive behavior skills for children and adolescents up to 18 years of age (Sparrow et al., 1984). The RARS is used because it is a standardized scale on a large sample of 220 patients with RTT.

5.1.1 Vineland Adaptive Behavior Scales

The VABS are designed to support the diagnosis of intellectual and developmental disabilities. The Scales are organized into four domains: communication; daily living; socialization; and motor skills. The interviewer asks general questions pertaining to the subject's functioning in each subdomain and uses the responses to rate the examinee on each critical behavior item (2: always present; 1: sometimes present; 0: seldom or never present). Typical interviews require approximately one hour. A total score is computed by summing the individual ratings for each scale. The reliability of the Scales was established as follows: split-half, 0.73–0.93 for the communication domain, 0.83–0.92 for daily living skills, 0.78–0.94 for socialization, 0.70–0.95 for motor skills, 0.84–0.98 for the adaptive behavior composite, 0.77–0.88 for maladaptive behavior (survey form) (0.80 and 0.90 for the Survey Form). The interrater reliability coefficients for the survey and expanded forms ranged from 0.62 to 0.75. Standard error of measurement ranged from 3.4 to 8.2 over the 4 domains, and from 2.2 to 4.9 for the Adaptive Behavior Composite, on the survey form. In the communication domain, an example of an item is the following: "Demonstrates understanding of the meaning of 'no' (for example, stops an ongoing activity or indicates knowledge that it should stop)". In the socialization domain, examples include asking for a play date or to go somewhere with another child. In the daily living domain, an example is the following: "Drinks from cup or glass unassisted (Some spilling while drinking may occur)". In the motor skills domain, examples include asking if the child walks down stairs with alternating feet, without assistance (the child may use a railing).

5.2 Rett Assessment Rating Scale

The structure of RARS is similar to that of CARS (the Childhood Autism Rating Scale), GARS (the Gilliam Autism Rating Scale) (Gilliam, 1995), and ASDS (Asperger Syndrome Diagnostic Scale), well-known instruments devised to assess the presence/absence of symptoms characterizing pervasive developmental disorders included in the same nosographic category as RTT (American Psychiatric Association, 2000).

The construction of the items of the scale was carried out following the diagnostic criteria for RTT proposed by the DSMIV-TR (American Psychiatric Association, 2000) and following recent research and clinical experience. A total of 30 items representative of the profile of RTT were devised. Each item concerns a specific phenotypic characteristic. It reports the description of four increasing levels of severity of the issue in question. Each item comes with a brief glossary that explains its meaning in a few words. Each item has to be rated on a 7-point scale as follows: 1 = within normal limits; 2 = infrequent or low abnormality; 3 = frequent or medium-high abnormality; 4 = strong abnormality. Intermediate rates can be endorsed (for example, when the answer is between point 2 and point 3, the 2.5 point has to be marked).

RARS allows evaluators to discriminate the level of severity of the clinical manifestations in a fine-grained manner, since each manifestation has to be evaluated on a 7-point scale (in comparison, for instance, to the 5-point scale employed in the Clinical Severity Score or to even fewer points in the other above-mentioned scales).

For each item, the evaluator has to circle the number that corresponds to the point that best describes the RTT patient. After a patient has been rated on each of the 30 items, a total score is computed by summing the individual ratings. This total score allows the evaluator to identify the level of severity of RTT, conceptualized as a continuum ranging from mild symptoms to severe deficits. Scores for each subscale are computed as well, by summing up the scores of each item belonging to the corresponding area (sensory, cognitive, and so on).

The RARS was obtained by a standardization procedure, involving a sample of 220 RTT patients, proving that the instrument is statistically valid and reliable (Vignoli et al., 2010). More precisely, normal distribution analyses of the scores were computed and the mean scores of the scale were similar to the median and to the mode. Skewness and kurtosis values, calculated for the distribution of the total score, were 0.110 and 0.352, respectively. The distribution was found to be normal. Cronbach's α was used to determine the internal consistency for the whole scale and subscales. Total α was 0.912, and the internal consistency of the subscales was high (α varying from 0.811 to 0.934). The following are examples of the items of RARS:

1. She normally uses nonverbal communication, which is appropriate considering her age and situation.
2. She uses a relatively mildly abnormal nonverbal communication. She may only point vaguely, or reach for what she wants, in situations where a child of the same age may point or gesture more specifically to indicate what he or she wants.
3. She uses moderately abnormal nonverbal communication. She is generally unable to express needs or desires nonverbally, and cannot understand the nonverbal communication of others.
4. She shows a severely abnormal use of nonverbal communication and shows no awareness of the meanings associated with the gestures or facial expressions of others (see Figure 5.1 & Appendix 5.1).

VI. Verbal communication:

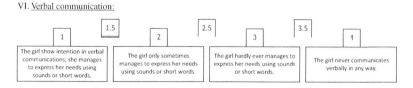

Figure 5.1 Example of items in the RARS.

5.3 Task analysis

Task analysis is used most often with those patients who have problems mastering complex behaviors (e.g., individuals with autism, people have an intellectual disability or are mentally ill, young children). Task analysis refers to what a user is required to do in terms of actions and/ or cognitive processes to achieve a task. The process of task analysis emerged from the behaviorist era in an effort to describe the elemental behaviors involved in performing a task or job. Nevertheless, with the transition from behaviorism to cognitive psychology and constructivism, different methods of task analysis have followed. Ultimately, each methodology of instruction commands its own method of analysis, yet regardless of methodology, a task analysis is needed for an in-depth understanding of the learning that's to take place. The method for analyzing tasks is task decomposition. The aim of high-level task decomposition is to decompose the high-level tasks and break them down into their constituent subtasks and operations. This will show an overall structure of the main user tasks. At a lower level, it may be desirable to show the task flows, decision processes, and even screen layouts (see task flow analysis in the text following). The process of task decomposition is best represented as a structure chart (similar to that used in Hierarchical Task Analysis). This shows the sequencing of activities by ordering them from left to right and from bottom to up. In order to break down a task, the question that should be asked is "how is this task done?" If a subtask is identified at a lower level, it is possible to build up the structure by asking "why is this done?" The task decomposition can be carried out using the following stages:

1. Identify the task to be analyzed.
2. Break this down into subtasks. These subtasks should be specified in terms of objectives and between them should cover the whole area of interest.
3. Draw the subtasks as a layered diagram, ensuring that it is complete.
4. Decide upon the level of detail into which to decompose the task. Making a conscious decision at this stage will ensure that all the subtask decompositions are treated consistently. It may be decided that the decomposition should continue until flows are more easily represented as a task flow diagram.
5. Continue the decomposition process, ensuring that the decompositions and numbering are consistent. It is usually helpful to produce a written account as well as the decomposition diagram.

6. Present the analysis to someone else who has not been involved in the decomposition, but who knows the tasks well enough to check for consistency.

Examples of task analysis may come from different areas: cognitive, behavioral, and emotional abilities. A method of systematic task analysis is applied to the problem of designing a sequence of learning objectives that will provide an optimal match for the child's natural sequence of acquisition of mathematical skills and concepts. An operational definition of the number concept is the form of a set of behaviors which, taken together, permit the inference that the child has an abstract concept of "number". These are the "objectives" of the curriculum. Each behavior in the defining set is then subjected to an analysis that identifies hypothesized components of skilled performance and prerequisites for learning these components. On the basis of these analyses, specific sequences of learning objectives are proposed. The proposed sequences are hypothesized to be those that will best facilitate learning, by maximizing transfer from earlier to later objectives. The paper concludes with a discussion of the ways in which the curriculum can be implemented and studied in schools. Examples of data on individual children are presented, and the use of such data for improving the curriculum itself, as well as for examining the effects of other treatment variables, is considered. In the following figure, the aim that a child has to reach is "count objects, moving them out of the set as he counts". We have to start from the bottom. Level IV specifies prerequisites, Level III a higher level of prerequisite abilities, Level II higher than this, and Level I is the aim (see Figure 5.2).

Another example comes from a behavioral analysis of making a cup of tea (see Figure 5.3).

The first phase, starting from the bottom, is to fill the tea kettle with water, place the kettle on the stove and bring to the boil, then turn off the gas. Then we have to follow the prerequisite abilities described in 1, 2, 3, 4, 5, and 6 and reach the objective.

Another type of task analysis is cognitive task analysis: it identifies aspects of system design that place heavy demands on the user's cognitive resources including memory, attention, and decision-making (Castelli et al., 2013; Fabio et al., 2018b, 2018c). It is used to determine thought processes that users follow to perform tasks at various levels, from novice to expert. Cognitive task analysis looks at the system from the viewpoint of the user performing a specific task. The

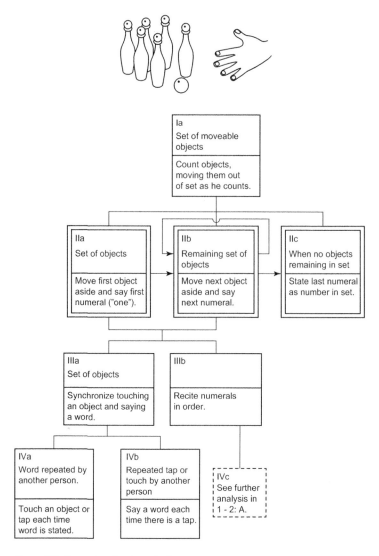

Figure 5.2 Example of task analysis.

information gathered allows the designer to focus upon the system features that the user will find hardest to learn and where he or she will be likely to make the most errors. Included in the analysis is an examination of past critical incidents that may have occurred to shape the user's feelings or expectations about the task. By identifying

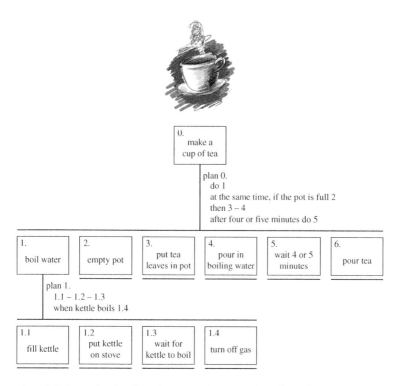

Figure 5.3 Example of task analysis to make a cup of tea (start from the bottom).

and highlighting where potential challenges could occur, designers can create a system that leaves more time for the user to perform the given task, rather than struggle with using the interface (Downs et al., 2010).

There are many different methods for conducting cognitive task analysis. At a minimum, cognitive task analysis should include the same steps of task analysis of mapping out the task, identifying the critical decision points, clustering, linking, and prioritizing them, and characterizing the strategies used. Cognitive task analysis relies on the technique of Data Driven Knowledge Elicitation (DDKE) to extract information about cognitive events, structures, and models. In-depth interviews are used to probe into the cognitive processes of users who are performing the task. However, interviews are often very subjective, so the data collected may not present a complete and accurate representation of the cognitive processes involved. To account for this bias, controlled observation methods are also recommended. Controlled observation uses verbal protocol analysis of an expert's responses to the task when instructed to think out loud. An advantage of controlled observation is that key features of the task can be manipulated and data can be automatically collected by the system.

We can make assessments of all behaviors of the person with whom we are working or we can also use assessments present in the specific literature, such as the Portage method or the Vineland Scales.

Assessment of both processes and abilities leads to defining cognitive, emotional, and behavioral objectives that are unique for each intellectually disabled person. For example, if we discover that a child is not able to turn off the gas, our proximal objective is to teach him how to do that. If we discover that he is able to read figures, but not symbols, our proximal objective is to teach him to read symbols. Aims are normally organized at three levels: behavioral, emotional, and cognitive.

In Appendix 5.2, we propose an example of a functional assessment of a child with Rett Syndrome.

5.4 Basic methods of cognitive empowerment

In this section, basic methods of cognitive empowerment will be presented. To begin with, unconditional acceptance of the child is considered. This is the most important concept for the development of the child. In the second part of the chapter, methods of cognitive empowerment are considered.

In educational intervention, the relationship with adults is based upon the following methods: unconditional acceptance, rules, reinforcement, containment, shaping, fading, prompting, hierarchy, automatic process, abstraction, and economy (Castelli et al., 2013; Fabio et al., 2013; Fabio et al., 2014; 2016; 2017) .

5.4.1 Unconditional acceptance

A prerequisite for growth is unconditional acceptance. Unconditional acceptance means that the child is supported in all that he is, no matter what that might be. This does not mean that the child is supported in acting out all that he is, rather that he is supported in expressing whatever he has inside, no matter what it is and no matter what it might trigger in the facilitator. Given unconditional acceptance, the child at some point begins likewise to unconditionally accept him/her-self – all of him/herself. When he/she begins to be able to do that, he/she has tipped the balance in favor of the real self and can be said to be more real than unreal. That is to say that a crucial element of the real self is its unconditional acceptance of itself, and a crucial element of the unreal self is its not-acceptance of the total self. The unreal self is that part of the personality embodying all the put-downs, negation, suppression, and harassment of the self that were original elements of the familial and social milieu of the developing individual. Thus, when the individual, in the educational relationship, begins to uncondition-ally accept all of him/herself, he/she can be said to be identifying more with the real self, an element of which is acceptance, than with the unreal self, the essence of which is non-acceptance (Feuerstein, Rand, & Rynders, 1988).

Unconditional acceptance is the indispensable element of a pri-mal therapy whose stated goal is to get people to be real. It may also be why some other therapies succeed, to an extent, in helping a person to be more real, in that they grant unconditional accept-ance. Meanwhile, some primal therapists sometimes fail in the same attempt, in that they facilitate abreaction, tension reduction, and con-nection, but are not able to grant unconditional acceptance of a cru-cial part of their client.

In schools, unconditional acceptance can be implemented through giving positive feedback to children with RTT. For example, the teacher can say: "I'm happy to meet you". Children with RTT per-ceive the level of acceptance that people have toward them, so it is very important that teacher and caregivers are disposed towards uncondi-tional acceptance of the students, to make them feel loved despite their difficulties in daily interactions.

5.4.2 Rules

Rules are very important keys in this intervention since they can con-vey order to the external world, which otherwise would be perceived as chaotic and disorganized/disrupted. Rules can work if they are con-stantly and repeatedly used in the right manner; rules must be few and given in an affirmative way ("keep your hands still", instead of "do not move your hands") and must be concrete and given at the right moment. For example, when a girl has hand stereotypies (hand wring-ing, tapping, and mouthing) during homework, we can tell her "you have to keep your hands steady" and gently help her to stop with our hands.

5.4.3 Reinforcement

Reinforcement occurs when an event following a response causes an increase in the probability of that response occurring in the future. Response strength can be assessed by measures such as the frequency with which the response happens (for example, a child may rise from the bench more times during the lesson), or the speed with which it happens (for example, the child may read a book page faster than another child). The environment change contingent upon the response is called a reinforcer. Reinforcers are nice events that may increase the probability that the subsequent behavior will be shown again. There are different types of reinforcement. A primary reinforcer is a stimulus that does not require pairing to function as a reinforcer and most likely has obtained this function through evolution and its role in the species' survival (Fabio et al., 2009; Fabio et al., 2011). For example, if a girl with RTT likes to eat, when she correctly chooses the target (a food), rather than another stimulus (cartoon), you can give her a biscuit or her favorite food. Examples of primary reinforcements include sleep, food, air, water, and sex. While these primary reinforcements are fairly stable through life and across individuals, the reinforcing value of different primary reinforcements varies due to multiple factors (e.g. genetics, experience). Thus, one person may prefer one type of food, while another abhors it. Or one person may eat lots of food, while another eats very little. So even though food is a primary reinforcer for both individuals, the value of food as a reinforcer differs between them (see Figure 5.4).

A secondary reinforcer is a stimulus or situation that has acquired its function as a reinforcer after pairing with a stimulus which functions as a reinforcer. This stimulus may be a primary reinforcer or

Figure 5.4 Examples of primary reinforcements.

Figure 5.5 Examples of secondary reinforcements.

another conditioned reinforcer (such as money). An example of a secondary reinforcer would be the sound from a door-bell. This sound has been associated with the appearance of a particular person, and subsequently, the sound may function as a reinforcer. As with primary reinforcements, an organism can experience satiation and deprivation with secondary reinforcements (see Figure 5.5).

An example of secondary reinforcement for girls with RTT is the following: when you ask a girl "please, open the door" and she tries to touch the door handle, afterwards you give her a hug or say "very good". Another example is when the girl chooses to listen to music by looking at a radio or a CD, we play a song or help her to dance.

Reinforcements are strictly personal, so it is necessary that educators know what events are nice for each student: for one student, it can be his favorite snack, for another one, his favorite songs, and so on.

5.4.4 Containment

Containment occurs when students present stereotypes, they should be bodily/physically contained to enhance their attention process. For instance, their hands have to be kept separate in order to interrupt hand stereotypes and their attention should be driven to the work to be done. For example, if the girl has a hand stereotypies (wringing, tapping, or mouthing) while she is watching TV, you can tell her "please stop and watch TV" by containing her hands. Another example is the educator putting his hands on the girl's hand to stop the stereotypies.

5.4.5 Shaping

Shaping or modeling consists of reinforcing every approximation that is similar to the desired behavior, until the student shows a

Figure 5.6 Example of verbal shaping.

meta-behavior (a behavior that is close to the desired one) that was not in his behavioral repertoire (Fox, 1986). Shaping involves gradually modifying the existing behavior into the desired behavior. If the student engages with a rabbit by hitting it, then he or she could have their behavior shaped by reinforcing interactions in which he or she touches the rabbit more gently. Over many interactions, successful shaping would replace the hitting behavior with patting or other gentler behavior (see Figure 5.6).

For example, if a girl with RTT is not able to touch an object, firstly, you can put her hands near the object (a bottle); secondly, you can move the object a little bit further away so that the girl has to move her arm more; thirdly, you move the object further until the girl shows a behavior that is close to the desired one (touch object).

5.4.6 Fading

Fading consists of giving a lot of help at the beginning of the work and then in gradually removing it, so that the student becomes able to do that work without any help. As an individual gains mastery of a skill at a particular prompt level, the prompt is faded to a less intrusive prompt. This ensures that the individual does not become overly dependent on a particular prompt when learning a new behavior or skill (see Figure 5.7 and Figure 5.8).

For example, if a girl with RTT is not able to drink using a glass, firstly, you can help her by holding the glass with your hands and secondly, you hold the glass with less help, and so on until the girl is able to do it without help.

Figure 5.7 Example of oural fading: initially, the father helps the child who cannot walk, then the parents give him only their hands, and finally he is able to run alone.

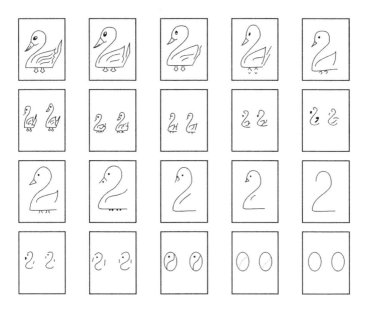

Figure 5.8 Example of fading on the "2" digit; initially two swans are presented, then step by step they become the "2" digit.

5.4.7 Prompting

A prompt is a cue or assistance to encourage the desired response from an individual. Prompts are often categorized into a prompt hierarchy from most intrusive to least intrusive. There is some controversy about what is considered most intrusive: physically intrusive versus hardest prompt to fade (i.e. verbal). In an errorless learning approach, prompts are given in a most-to-least sequence and faded systematically to ensure the individual experiences a high level of success. There may be instances in which a least-to-most prompt method is preferred. Prompts are faded systematically and as quickly as possible to avoid prompt dependency. The goal of teaching using prompts would be to fade prompts towards independence, so that no prompts are needed for the individual to perform the desired behavior.

Types of prompts:

1. Verbal prompts: utilizing a vocalization to indicate the desired response.
2. Visual prompts: a visual cue or picture.

3. Gestural prompts: utilizing a physical gesture to indicate the desired response.
4. Positional prompt: the target item is placed closer to the individual.
5. Modeling: modeling the desired response for the student. This type of prompt is best suited for individuals who learn through imitation and can attend to a model.
6. Physical prompts: physically manipulating the individual to produce the desired response. There are many degrees of physical prompts, the most intrusive being hand-over-hand, and the least intrusive being a slight tap to initiate movement.

When using prompts to systematically teach a skill, not all prompts need to be used in the hierarchy; prompts are chosen based on which ones are most effective for a particular individual.

5.4.8 Hierarchy

Hierarchy means to learn from simplest objectives to more complex ones. As presented in the example in Chapter 2, a child has to learn the + (plus) sign first, and when he masters it, he can move on to learning the × (multiplication) sign (see Figure 5.9).

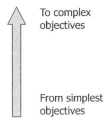

To complex
objectives

From simplest
objectives

Figure 5.9 The hierarchy process.

5.4.9 Automatism

Automatism refers to the dynamics from controlled processing to automatic processing of attention. In any starting step of a task, we initially use controlled processes of attention to learn and so performance is slow, awkward, and prone to errors. We can say that the full amount of our memory load is engaged; we can say, in other words, that all our cognitive resources are engaged to learn the new task.

For example, we can think of a child who is learning to add up two numbers. It is very difficult initially for the child to bear in mind the first number, to memorize the second number, to recall the first, and to sum both. It is difficult also to understand that the plus sign means "to add", "to join", but also "become bigger", "go on", and so on. So, when the teacher asks the child to add the toys of Mary to the toys of Marc, he thinks hard, he does it slowly, and then reaches the result. During his problem solving, if someone asks him something else, he makes mistakes in the calculation and forgets the result. As training proceeds, the performance requires less vigilance, becomes faster, and errors decrease, a transformation that can be defined as "automatism". With learning, the attentive strategies that once needed control become automatic (Caprì et al., 2019; Fabio & Caprì, 2015; 2017; 2019; Fabio, Castriciano, & Rondanini, 2015; Martino et al., 2017).

Coming back to the previously-mentioned child, as his learning proceeds, he becomes able to think of the plus sign faster and reaches the result easily. He also becomes able to reply to someone who asks him something else. In other words, the child automates his learning of the plus sign. We are positioned in the A level, when automatism appears and the discharge of cognitive load on A level takes place.

Later, the child has to learn how to multiply, or how to sum up and subtract some quantity. If he were totally (or even partially) engaged in the A level, it would be difficult to access more complex tasks. He can now have access to the execution of subtraction and summing up (B level), thanks to the fact that he assumed the A level as an automatic subroutine.

With reference to RTT, when you teach a child with RTT to read the word "dad", you have to present the word "dad" several times, until the child looks at this word and combines it with her father's picture. This method allows us to move to a more complex level, for example "dad reads". Only when the child understands the single word "dad" can she recognize units composed of more words.

5.4.10 Abstraction

Abstraction refers to the passage leading from concrete experience to symbolization. In effect, it is important that learning involves not only symbolic learning, but also concrete learning. To understand the symbolic value of the concept of numerical quantity, a child has to be trained beforehand in counting concrete materials and things. For example, if you want to teach a child with RTT the use of the number four, you first show four candies to the child and you help the child to touch them

Figure 5.10 Abstraction: from the concrete quantity to symbol "3".

with her hand. After this, you present four pictures of balls and you help her to touch these balls. Then you present an image of a chair (this object is similar to the number four), and at the end, you present the picture of the number four (see Figure 5.10).

5.4.11 Economy

Economy refers to the fact that in any learning setting, it is better to try to give the smallest possible help, so that the subject is stimulated to autonomy. Sometimes educators help learners too much which prevents them from becoming independent of the educator.

While RTT has no cure, research suggests that intervention begun soon after the diagnosis offers the greatest chance of producing a positive impact on skills in later years. The earlier the treatment starts, the better the possibility for learning, as well as managing other problems developed by individuals with Rett Syndrome.

5.5 Motor intervention

In this section, we describe motor intervention on walking. The interventions aimed at improving or regaining lost walking ability in the girls with RTT represent a way to enhance the environmental conditions in which these girls and their families live.

Downs and colleagues (2010) developed guidelines for the clinical management of scoliosis in RTT through evidence review, consensus expert panel opinion, and the perspectives of parents. An international and multidisciplinary panel of clinicians participated in a modified Delphi technique. These clinicians come from different countries in the disciplines of orthopedics, spinal surgery, pediatrics, pediatric neurology, clinical genetics, anesthesia, nursing, and physical and occupational therapy. The project of Downs and colleagues (2010) was aimed at responding to questions of parents about the management of scoliosis.

With reference to monitoring and intervention prior to the diagnosis of scoliosis, the guidelines suggested the following practical directions (Downs et al., 2010):

1. All children with a clinical diagnosis of RTT should have a molecular test as the genotype may influence the development and management of scoliosis;
2. Children with abnormal early development and those who never learned to walk have been shown to be at higher risk of developing scoliosis;
3. A physical assessment of the spine should be conducted at the time of diagnosis of RTT;
4. A physical assessment of the spine should be conducted at least every six months after diagnosis of RTT;
5. Develop, maintain, and promote walking for as long as possible;
6. Maintain the strength of the back extensors and the flexibility of the spine;
7. Implement a postural management scheme that includes appropriate support for the correct sitting posture and sleeping posture supports;
8. Families should be given information about scoliosis early in the child's clinical course.

With reference to practical matters for scoliosis and spinal bracing, the guidelines suggested the following directions (Downs et al., 2010):

1. Physiotherapy should be used to maintain general wellbeing in children with RTT and scoliosis; it does not prevent the progression of an established curvature;
2. Increase the distance that the child can walk;
3. Increase the length of time that the child is able to stand on her feet;
4. Maintain a range of movement of joints;
5. Walking and/or standing at least two hours per day;
6. For those who cannot walk, support standing in a standing frame for at least 30 minutes a day;
7. Symmetrical supported seating is valuable for the child's comfort and functioning;
8. Time spent in daylight and/or supplements of vitamin D should be considered to promote bone health;

9. Improving dietary intake of calcium should be considered to promote bone health;
10. In severe scoliosis where surgery is not indicated, the management plan should include the provision of supported sitting to optimize posture;
11. In severe scoliosis where surgery is not indicated, the management plan should include the monitoring and treatment of pressure sores;
12. In severe scoliosis where surgery is not indicated, the management plan should include chest physiotherapy, flu immunization, and a low threshold for antibiotic use to minimize the effects of restrictive lung disease.

In conclusion, the guidelines summarized previously incorporate a comprehensive approach to multiple aspects of health in subjects with RTT and motor abilities and can be used by both clinicians and caregivers (Downs et al., 2010).

5.6 New rehabilitation strategies

According to new knowledge, innovative techniques in the rehabilitation field are spreading, such as non-invasive cerebral stimulation. The procedures of neurostimulation evoke specific excitatory or inhibitory responses, in a short pause (milliseconds or seconds) from the ending of the application of energy. They are able to induce effects during the stimulation or effects that last after the end of the stimulation.

The neurostimulation techniques can influence specific parts of the brain by activation or inhibition of their functionality. Many neurological and psychiatric disorders are correlated to a hyperfunction or hypofunction of specific areas of the nervous system; neurostimulation methods represent a therapeutic possibility which is based on the principle of the normalization of the activity in the dysfunctional areas. Hence, we talk about "neuromodulation" i.e. the application of neurostimulation techniques with the aim to reactivate the normal activity or function of specific dysfunctional areas or structures of the brain.

A number of promising interventions targeted towards promoting neuroplasticity have been identified. These forms of interventions include an appreciation of learning theory, Hebbian principles, task-specific training, social influences, mechanisms of verbal encoding, and the interplay across brain modalities. In recent years, within the landscape of cognitive neuroscience, new technologies that facilitate synaptogenesis processes in patients with brain injury or neurodegenerative diseases have evolved.

Several forms of non-invasive brain stimulation have been examined as a possibility for changing brain function and thereby promoting neuroplasticity. Within neuromodulatory techniques, transcranial direct current stimulation (tDCS) has been analyzed with three girls with Rett Syndrome (Fabio et al., 2018a).

In tDCS stimulation, the cerebral cortex is stimulated through a weak DC current in a noninvasive and painless manner. tDCS stimulation can be applied specifically and selectively to defined cortical regions, particularly when guided by neuroimaging and physiological measures. During tDCS administration, a small electrical current passes through brain structures via electrodes placed on the scalp. This current is insufficient for the neuronal depolarization; rather, it is considered to induce incremental shifts in the resting membrane potential of large numbers of neurons under the electrodes.

These modest shifts in the resting state are sufficient to drive measurable changes in neurophysiology and cognitive functions (Nitsche & Paulus, 2013).

Several studies have shown that this technique modulates cortical excitability in the human motor and visual cortex; that its modulatory effect remains after stimulation if tDCS is applied for several minutes; that tDCS not only shifts the activity of cortical areas situated directly under the electrodes, but also of distant areas, probably by interconnections of the primary stimulated area with these structures.

The effects of tDCS have been observed up to an hour following a single stimulation session and may persist for days or even months after multiple days of stimulation (Reis et al., 2009). It is believed that the polarity of the electrodes determines their effects on cortical activity. Anodal-stimulation has been associated with facilitative effects on cortical activity, while cathodal-stimulation has been associated with inhibitory effects.

Nitsche and colleagues (2013) identified as the mechanism at the basis of the tDCS its ability to modify the polarization of the neuronal membrane, because of which the anodic stimulation would provoke an increase of the spontaneous neuronal activity consequent to the depolarization of the membrane. In their experiment, the authors identified the areas which were needed to be stimulated through the transcranial magnetic stimulation (TMS), so they fixed the electrodes (size: 35 cm²) on such areas, the cathode on the left area representing the minor adductor muscle of the pollex, the anode on the contralateral orbital cortex supplying a current intensity of 1mA. They successively measured the motor evoke potentials (MEPs), discovering that the effects of the stimulation were longer than the stimulation itself in a proportional way to its intensity and duration. The two researchers believed that the genesis of such phenomenon was the mechanisms of the long-term potentiation (LTP) and the long-term depression (LTD).

Another experiment used the same parameters as Nitsche and Paulus, revealing that the anodic stimulation left the level of spontaneous activation almost unaltered and that meanwhile, the cathodic stimulation provoked a strong decrease in the MEPs.

The studies that followed revealed the mechanisms underlying the long-term effects of the tDCS. Ardolino and colleagues (2005) conducted an experiment on 17 healthy right-handed subjects. They applied the cathodic electrode on the right motor area and the anodic electrode on the upper left orbital area, one on the wrist in direction of the ulnar nerve, and the other one on the ipsilateral knee. In this way, they wanted to investigate the long-lasting effects of the direct currents needs synapse, as the model of peripheral stimulation does not involve the synapsis, but only the axonal excitability. In the experiment, transcranial magnetic stimulation (TMS), electrical stimulation (TES) and the electroencephalogram (EEG), and the registration of the motor evoked potentials (MEPs) were applied. The results demonstrated that the cathodic stimulation produces long-lasting and functional effects, both on the central nervous system and on the peripheral nervous system, causing changes in the peripheral axonal excitability, in the polarization of the neuronal membrane, and in the extent of the motor evoked potentials (MEPs). However, the changes in the axonal excitement of the peripheral nervous system were in the inverse direction to the one of the central nervous system; indeed, after the cathodic stimulation, the axonal excitability was not decreased, but increased.

The aim of a recent study by Fabio and colleagues (2018a) was to examine the neurophysiological and cognitive effects of Transcranial Direct Current Stimulation (tDCS) in three girls with RTT with chronic language impairments. They applied an integrated intervention: tDCS and cognitive empowerment applied to language in order to enhance speech production (new functional sounds and new words). Because maximal gains usually are achieved when tDCS is coupled with behavioral training, they applied tDCS stimulation on Broca's area together with linguistic training. The results indicated a general enhancement in language abilities (an increase in the number of vowel/consonant sounds and words and the production and comprehension through discrimination), motor coordination (functional movements), and neurophysiological parameters (an increase in the frequency and power of alpha, beta, and theta bands). Fabio and colleagues (2018a) assume that tDCS stimulation combined with the cognitive empowerment applied to language can significantly influence a chronic impairment, even in genetic syndromes. The results provide data that support the role of tDCS in fostering brain plasticity, and in particular, in empowering speech production and comprehension in girls with RTT.

Advances in science and technology are providing opportunities for innovative approaches in the rehabilitation of RTT through computer-based cognitive training programs. Benefits of these programs include high user engagement and a low-cost extension of treatment beyond the clinical setting, care, and maintenance. Moreover, advances in neuroplasticity-based research suggest that highly repetitive, adaptive, novel, and targeted stimuli can enhance brain performance. For these reasons, novel brain training treatment tools and computer-based training continue to emerge on the cognitive and motor rehabilitation in RTT. Currently, the literature on cognitive rehabilitation and motor training in RTT is based on operant conditioning principles and on the Feuerstein approach. Despite results of clinical studies in the rehabilitation of RTT generally showing significant effects, evidence is needed for the efficacy and feasibility of implementing new programs using multiple treatment methods.

5.6.1 Eye-tracker Tobii Series

Nowadays, eye-tracking technology is well-known and it is reasonable to use it in medical purposes, especially in supporting the assessment of patients with serious communication barriers. More precisely, eye-tracking technology is used in cognitive rehabilitation for people with RTT.

Eye-tracker records the subject's visual scanning response to a cognitive task implemented in the device. Specifically, it records ocular movements such as the location and duration of ocular fixations (i.e., pause of eye movement on an object of interest) and saccadic movements (i.e., rapid movements between fixations). Overall, the subject is positioned at a distance of about 30 cm from the screen and the direction of the gaze is determined according to the Pupil Center/Corneal Reflection Method of low-intensity infrared light. Passive gaze tracing

(LCTechnologies, Sao Paulo, Brazil) software is used to generate gaze data during visual scanning. Sensory eye FX is a set of 30 software applications designed for the earliest level of eye-gaze computer access.

In a study by Vignoli and colleagues (2010), eye-tracker was used to measure recognition, matching of pairs (the same), and semantic categorization (the similar). Three tasks were designed: (1) response to verbal instruction (look at the dog, etc.); (2) recognition and matching of pairs (look at the one that is the same); and (3) semantic categorization (look at the one that is similar). The images used were of objects familiar to the children, according to their parents. Nine different pictures were divided into three groups: fruit – apple, orange, and banana; animals – dog, cat, and horse; and emotions – happy, sad, and angry. Each item was presented for five seconds. The parameter was the length (seconds) of fixation i.e. eye-tracker parameters. The Eyegaze device was used to record the subject's visual scanning response to visual computer screen stimulation. This study suggested that eye-tracking was a valid instrument to record the visual scan response to a cognitive task in RTT.

Another study by Fabio and colleagues (2016) used the eye-tracker technology to measure the visual scan response to a cognitive task. The aim of this study was to investigate whether behaviors and brain activity were modified by training in RTT. The modifications were assessed in two phases: (1) after a short-term training (STT) session i.e. after 30 minutes of training and (2) after long-term training (LTT) i.e. after 5 days of training. This research demonstrated the efficacy of eye-tracking technology as a valid instrument in the rehabilitation of RTT.

Baptista and colleagues (2006) demonstrated that intentional gaze is a measurable parameter in girls with RTT and can be used to explore their cognitive performance. More recently, the same authors recommended reevaluation of the method because a small group of 10 girls with RTT (aged 4–12 years) did not manifest recognition of the solicited concepts within a fixation time of 4 seconds, even if they argued that the low age of the sample and the brief fixation span could have interfered with the results. Although it is well known that girls with RTT have good visual attention, it has recently been shown that they are able to learn to discriminate complex stimuli; however, they have a specific deficit in the ability to attend selectively to relevant sources of information while ignoring irrelevant ones.

In conclusion, the aforementioned studies support the use of eye-tracking as an assistive tool, especially as a tool for alternative communication and cognition. We suggest that eye-tracking technology might be useful in several steps of the rehabilitation process, from diagnosis to therapeutic implications, especially when eyeball movement is the only channel of communication, as for people with RTT.

5.7 Conclusion

As seen in this book, RTT is a complex disorder with a big variety of symptoms. Subjects with RTT have minimal opportunities to interact constructively with their environment, show reduced sensory input, very limited mobility, and usually experience low levels of quality of life. The complexity of the disease makes it very hard for staff to apply conventional rehabilitation programs aimed at developing positive engagement and improving their mood (Lancioni et al., 2005). Thus, there is a need for novel evidence-based approaches for treating cognitive and motor symptoms of individuals with RTT. Numerous reviews summarize the evidence for the effectiveness of traditional cognitive and motor rehabilitation with some specific interventions showing moderate or strong evidence for efficacy. Despite results in cognitive rehabilitation generally showing a positive trend, the efficacy of specific intervention is less consolidated in some fields, for example, articulated speech. Likewise, a certain number of studies demonstrate the improvment or regaining of lost walking ability in subjects with RTT, but following intensive intervention (Lotan & Hanks, 2006). Evidence-based reviews suggest that the most efficacious approach to rehabilitation for subjects with RTT is comprehensive day-treatment programs that include individual sessions for several hours per day. Several works also show that these intensive programs are effective in improving rehabilitation outcomes, including cognitive and motor skills. However, there is a lack of studies on integrated intervention with motor and cognitive training in individuals with RTT employing new technology (Stasolla et al., 2015). The literature on the use of new technologies in people with neurological disabilities is encouraging, although studies on this field are still limited in the population with RTT (Fabio et al., 2019; Murdaca, Fabio, & Caprì, 2018; Lancioni et al., 2004; 2005; 2006; Stasolla et al., 2015).

To our knowledge, little research has employed an integrated intervention that combines motor and cognitive training applied to people with RTT. Given the complexity and range of symptoms experienced by people with RTT in both cognitive and motor domains, it is important to recognize that these domains of functioning interact. Consequently, interventions directed at only, or primarily, one domain may be confounded by this interaction. To maximize treatment potential, we believe rehabilitation for RTT has to integrate both cognitive and motor interventions. We also support the importance of incorporating both cognitive and motor interventions to enhance generalization of learned skills to community activities.

References

American Psychiatric Association (2000). *Diagnostic and Statistical Manual of Mental Disorders* (4th ed. text rev.). Washington, DC: American Psychiatric Association.

Baptista, P.M., Mercadante, M.T., Macedo, E.C. & Schwartzman, J.S. (2006). Cognitive performance in Rett syndrome girls: A pilot study using eye tracking technology. *Journal of Intellectual Disabilities Research, 50,* 662–666.

Caprì, T., Martino, G., Giannatiempo, S., Semino, M. & Fabio, R.A. (2019). Attention, problem solving and decision making in adult subjects with ADHD. *Journal of Clinical & Developmental Psychology, 1*(1), 1–9.

Castelli, I., Antonietti, A., Fabio, R.A., Lucchini, B. & Marchetti, A. (2013). Do Rett syndrome girls possess Theory of Mind? Some evidence from not-treated girls. *Life Span and Disability, XVI*(2), 157–168.

Downs, J., Bebbington, A., Jacoby, P., Williams, A.M., Ghosh, S., Kaufmann, W.E. & Leonard, H. (2010). Level of purposeful hand function as a marker of clinical severity in Rett syndrome. *Developmental Medicine Child Neurology, 52,* 817–823.

Fabio, R.A., Antonietti, A., Castelli, I. & Marchetti, A. (2009). Attention and communication in Rett Syndrome. *Research in Autism Spectrum Disorders, 3*(2), 329–335.

Fabio, R.A., Billeci, L., Crifaci, G., Troise, E., Tortorella, G. & Pioggia, G. (2016). Cognitive training modifies frequency EEG bands and neuropsychological measures in Rett syndrome. *Research in Developmental Disabilities, 54,* 73–85.

Fabio, R.A. & Caprì, T. (2015). Autobiographical memory in ADHD subtypes. *Journal of Intellectual and Developmental Disability, 40,* 26–36.

Fabio, R.A. & Caprì, T. (2017). The executive functions in a sample of Italian adults with ADHD: attention, response inhibition and planning/organization. *Mediterranean Journal of Clinical Psychology, 5*(3), 1–17.

Fabio, R.A. & Caprì, T. (2019). Automatic and controlled attentional capture by threatening stimuli. *Heliyon, 5,* 17–52.

Fabio, R.A., Caprì, T., Nucita, A., Iannizzotto, G. & Mohammadhasani, N. (2019). The role of eye gaze digital games to improve motivational and attentional ability in Rett syndrome. *Journal of Special Education and Rehabilitation*, 9(3–4), 105–126.

Fabio, R.A., Cardile, S., Troise, E., Polimeni, S., Germanò E., Di Rosa, G., Siracusano, R., Nicotera, A., Gagliano, A. & Tortorella, G. (2017). Cognitive empowerment with new technologies improves neuropsychological and neurophysiological parameters in Rett syndrome. In *Horizons in Neuroscience Research*, vol. 28, 199–217, A. Costa & E. Villalba. New York: Nova Science Publisher.

Fabio, R.A., Castelli, I., Marchetti, A. & Antonietti, A. (2013). Training communication abilities in Rett Syndrome through reading and writing. *Frontiers in Psychology*, 4, 9–11.

Fabio, R.A., Castriciano, C. & Rondanini, A. (2015). Auditory and visual stimuli in automatic and controlled processes. *Journal of Attention Disorders*, 19, 771–778.

Fabio, R.A., Colombo, B., Russo, S., Cogliati, F., Masciadri, M., Foglia, S., Antonietti, A. & Tavian, D. (2014). Recent insights into genotype-phenotype relationships in patients with Rett syndrome using a fine grain scale. *Research in Developmental Disabilities*, 35(11), 2976–2986.

Fabio, R.A., Gangemi, A., Capri, T., Budden, S. & Falzone, A. (2018a). Neurophysiological and cognitive effects of Transcranial Direct Current Stimulation in three girls with Rett Syndrome with chronic language impairments. *Research in Developmental Disabilities*, 76, 76–87.

Fabio, R.A., Giannatiempo, S., Antonietti, A. & Budden, S. (2009). The role of stereotypies in overselectivity process in Rett syndrome. *Research in Developmental Disabilities*, 30(1), 136–145.

Fabio, R.A., Giannatiempo, S., Oliva, P. & Murdaca, A.M. (2011). The increase of attention in Rett syndrome: a pre-test/post-test research design. *Journal of Developmental and Physical Disabilities*, 23(2), 99–111.

Fabio, R.A., Magaudda, C., Caprì, T., Towey, G.E. & Martino, G. (2018b). Choice behavior in Rett Syndrome: the consistency parameter. *Life Span and Disability*, 21(1), 47–62.

Fabio, R.A., Martino, G., Caprì, T., Giacchero, R., Giannatiempo, S., La Briola, F., Banderali, G., Canevini M.P. & Vignoli, A. (2018c). Long chain poly-unsaturated fatty acid supplementation in Rett Syndrome: a randomized placebo-controlled trial. *Asian Journal of Clinical Nutrition*, 10, 37–46.

Feuerstein, R., Rand, Y. & Rynders, J. (1988). *Don't Accept me as I am Helping Retarded People to Excel*. Baltimore, MD: University Park Press.

Gilliam, J.E. (1995). *Gilliam Autism Rating Scale (GARS)*. Austin, TX: Pro-Ed.

Lancioni, G.E., O'Reilly, M.F., Singh, N.N., Oliva, D., Baccani, S., Severini, L. & Groeneweg, J. (2006). Microswitch programmes for students with multiple disabilities and minimal motor behavior: assessing response acquisition and choice. *Pediatric Rehabilitation*, 9, 137–143.

Lancioni, G.E., O'Reilly, M.F., Singh, N.N., Oliva, D., Coppa, M.M. & Montironi, G. (2005). A new microswitch to enable a boy with minimal motor behavior to control environmental stimulation with eye blinks. *Behavioral Interventions*, 20, 147–153.

Lancioni, G.E., Singh, N.N., O'Reilly, M.F., Oliva, D., Montironi, G., Piazza, F., Ciavattini, E. & Bettarelli, F. (2004). Using computer systems as microswitches for vocal utterances of persons with multiple disabilities. *Research in Developmental Disabilities*, 25, 183–192.

Lotan, M. & Hanks, S. (2006). Physical therapy intervention for individuals with Rett syndrome. *The Scientific World Journal*, 6, 1314–1338.

Martino, G., Caprì, T., Castriciano, C. & Fabio, R.A. (2017). Automatic deficits can lead executive deficits in ADHD. *Mediterranean Journal of Clinical Psychology*, 5(3), 1–32.

Murdaca, A.M., Fabio, R.A. & Caprì, T. (2018). The use of new technologies to improve attention in neurodevelopmental disabilities: New educational scenarios for the enhancement of differences. *International Journal of Digital Literacy and Digital Competence*, 9(4), 46–57.

Nitsche, M.A., Liebetanz, D., Antal, A., Lang, N., Tergau, F. & Paulus, W. (2013). Modulation of cortical excitability by weak direct current stimulation-technical: Safety and functional aspects. *Supplements to Clinical Neurophysiology*, 56, 255–276.

Reis, J., Schambra, H.M., Cohen, L.G., Buch, E.R., Fritsch, B., Zarahn, E., et al. (2009). Noninvasive cortical stimulation enhances motor skill acquisition over multiple days through an effect on consolidation. *Proceedings of the National Academy of Sciences of the United States of America*, 106, 1590–1595.

Sparrow, S., Balla, D. & Cicchetti, D.V. (1984). *The Vineland Adaptive Behavior Scales (Survey form)*. Circle Pines, MN: American Guidance Service.

Stasolla, F., Perilli, V., Di Leone, A., Damiani, R., Albano, V., Stella, A. & Damato, C. (2015). Technological aids to support choice strategies by three girls with Rett syndrome. *Research in Developmental Disabilities*, 36, 36–44.

Vignoli, A., Fabio, R.A., La Briola, F., Giannatiempo, S., Antonietti, A., Maggiolini, S. & Canevini, M.P. (2010). Correlations between neurophysiological, behavioral, and cognitive function in Rett syndrome. *Epilepsy & Behavior*, 17, 489–496.

Appendix 5A.1: R.A.R.S. (Rett Assessment Rating Scale)

R.A.R.S. is a tool developed to assess the level of seriousness of the illness in girls suffering from Rett syndrome. It comprises 31 points concerning the various behavioural areas, each of which will be assigned a variable score from 1 to 4. The sum total of the scores will give an overall value determining a slight, average or high seriousness of Rett syndrome.

Cognitive Area
  I. Attention:

  II. Spatial orientation:

  III. Temporal orientation:

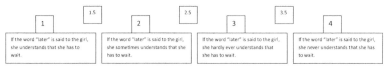

  IV. Memory:

  V. Eye contact, replying by smiling, shared attention:

VI. Verbal communication:

1	1.5	2	2.5	3	3.5	4
The girl show intention in verbal communications; she manages to express her needs using sounds or short words.		The girl only sometimes manages to express her needs using sounds or short words.		The girl hardly ever manages to express her needs using sounds or short words.		The girl never communicates verbally in any way.

VII. Non-verbal communication:

1	1.5	2	2.5	3	3.5	4
The girl normally uses non-verbal communication; she knows how to express herself using gestures and facial expressions.		The girl has difficulty in non-verbal communication; she manages to point and reach out to what she wants with her hand but only inaccurately.		The girl manages to point and reach out to what she wants only inaccurately and only sometimes.		The girl generally cannot express her needs or wishes in a non-verbal manner.

Sensoral Area
VIII. Eyesight:

1	1.5	2	2.5	3	3.5	4
Visual response is in the norm with respect to age and is used as a means of exploring new objects and there is a fixed look towards objects.		Visual response is not within the norm with respect to age; it is not always used as a means of exploring new objects and there is not always a fixed look towards objects.		The girl uses an intermittent and peripheral look (does not look directly at objects, but does so from out of the corner of the eye), recognising the difference between known and unknown objects.		The girl seems not to recognise the difference between known and unknown objects when looking at them.

IX. Hearing:

1	1.5	2	2.5	3	3.5	4
Hearing response is in the norm with respect to age and is used as a means of exploring the surrounds.		Hearing response is not in the norm with respect to age and is not always used as a means of exploring the surrounds.		Hearing response varies; the girl alternates periods of hypersensitive hearing with moments of very low hearing (she recognises aural stimulus as being very strong or not at all).		The girl has an excessive or no reaction to sounds, independently of their type.

Motorial Area
X. Body:

1	1.5	2	2.5	3	3.5	4
The girl is able to maintain an erect position and to walk by herself. She knows how to look where she is going, walk on any surface and go up and down stairs.		The girl is able to maintain an erect position but sometimes needs support when walking.		The girl is able to maintain an erect position but always needs support when walking.		The girl is unable to maintain an erect position or walk by herself. She needs a wheelchair or a pram in order to move around.

XI. Hands:

1	1.5	2	2.5	3	3.5	4
Functional use of the hands is only slightly affected; the girl manages to grip and hold objects for long enough to enable her to make ample movements. She has good hand-eye coordination. Stereotypes to not influence the intentional use of the hands.		Functional use of the hands is more compromised; the girl manages to touch, push or hit objects but not to grip them. Hand-eye coordination is scarce. The girl is inhibited in moving by stereotypes.		Functional use of the hands is compromised; the girl is not always able to use her hands intentionally; she does not always manage to touch objects, even if strongly motivated to do so, especially in the presence of marked stereotypes.		Functional use of the hands is almost completely compromised; the girl is not able to use her hands intentionally; she does not manage to touch objects even if strongly motivated to do so, especially because of insistent stereotypes.

XII. Scoliosis:

1	1.5	2	2.5	3	3.5	4
The girl shows no signs of scoliosis.		The girl shows signs of minor scoliosis.		The girl shows signs of major scoliosis.		The girl shows signs of very serious scoliosis.

XIII. Feet:

1	1.5	2	2.5	3	3.5	4
The girl has no problems with her feet.		The girl has slightly small feet, with minor circulation problems.		The girl has small, valgus or different sized feet, with circulation problems.		The girl has problems with her feet, to the extent that she is unable to walk.

Basic Emotions
XIV. Basic emotions:

1	1.5	2	2.5	3	3.5	4
The girl has no difficulty in expressing her basic emotions (happiness, anger, fear, sadness) through visual expressions, body language and emotive expressions.		The girl has some difficulty in expressing her basic emotions (happiness, anger, fear, sadness) through visual expressions, body language and emotive expressions.		The girl has major difficulty in expressing her basic emotions (happiness, anger, fear, sadness) through visual expressions, body language and emotive expressions.		The girl is unable to express her emotions.

XV. Others emotions:

1	1.5	2	2.5	3	3.5	4
The girl has no difficulty in understanding others emotions.		The girl has some difficulty in understanding others emotions.		The girl has major difficulty in understanding others emotions.		The girl is unable to understand others emotions.

Autonomy
XVI. Control of the sphincter:

1	1.5	2	2.5	3	3.5	4
The girl has full control of her excretive functions.		The girl is not always able to control her excretive functions.		The girl only has part control of her excretive functions; she needs help.		The girl has no control of her excretive functions.

XVII. Feeding:

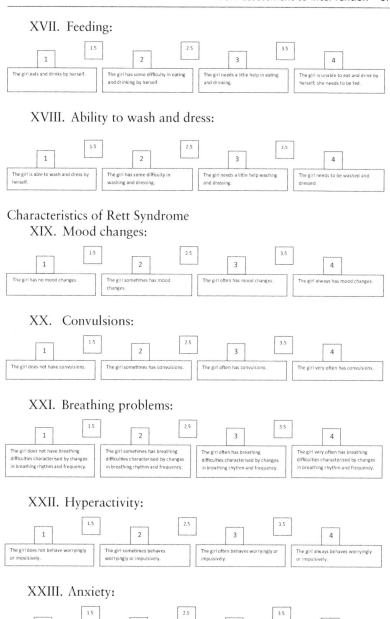

	1.5		2.5		3.5	
1		**2**		**3**		**4**
The girl eats and drinks by herself.		The girl has some difficulty in eating and drinking by herself.		The girl needs a little help in eating and drinking.		The girl is unable to eat and drink by herself; she needs to be fed.

XVIII. Ability to wash and dress:

	1.5		2.5		3.5	
1		**2**		**3**		**4**
The girl is able to wash and dress by herself.		The girl has some difficulty in washing and dressing.		The girl needs a little help washing and dressing.		The girl needs to be washed and dressed.

Characteristics of Rett Syndrome
XIX. Mood changes:

	1.5		2.5		3.5	
1		**2**		**3**		**4**
The girl has no mood changes.		The girl sometimes has mood changes.		The girl often has mood changes.		The girl always has mood changes.

XX.   Convulsions:

	1.5		2.5		3.5	
1		**2**		**3**		**4**
The girl does not have convulsions.		The girl sometimes has convulsions.		The girl often has convulsions.		The girl very often has convulsions.

XXI. Breathing problems:

	1.5		2.5		3.5	
1		**2**		**3**		**4**
The girl does not have breathing difficulties characterised by changes in breathing rhythm and frequency.		The girl sometimes has breathing difficulties characterised by changes in breathing rhythm and frequency.		The girl often has breathing difficulties characterised by changes in breathing rhythm and frequency.		The girl very often has breathing difficulties characterised by changes in breathing rhythm and frequency.

XXII. Hyperactivity:

	1.5		2.5		3.5	
1		**2**		**3**		**4**
The girl does not behave worryingly or impulsively.		The girl sometimes behaves worryingly or impulsively.		The girl often behaves worryingly or impulsively.		The girl always behaves worryingly or impulsively.

XXIII. Anxiety:

	1.5		2.5		3.5	
1		**2**		**3**		**4**
The girl does not have anxiety attacks.		The girl sometimes has anxiety attacks.		The girl often has anxiety attacks.		The girl always has anxiety attacks.

XXIV. Aggressiveness:

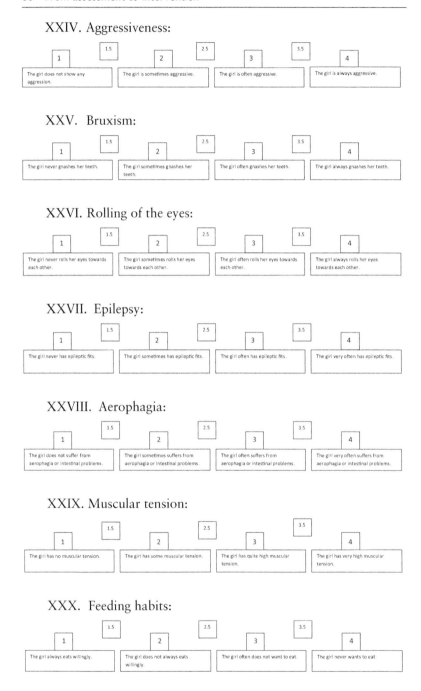

1.5		2.5		3.5	
1	2	3	4
The girl does not show any aggression.	The girl is sometimes aggressive.	The girl is often aggressive.	The girl is always aggressive.

XXV. Bruxism:

1.5		2.5		3.5	
1	2	3	4
The girl never gnashes her teeth.	The girl sometimes gnashes her teeth.	The girl often gnashes her teeth.	The girl always gnashes her teeth.

XXVI. Rolling of the eyes:

1.5		2.5		3.5	
1	2	3	4
The girl never rolls her eyes towards each other.	The girl sometimes rolls her eyes towards each other.	The girl often rolls her eyes towards each other.	The girl always rolls her eyes towards each other.

XXVII. Epilepsy:

1.5		2.5		3.5	
1	2	3	4
The girl never has epileptic fits.	The girl sometimes has epileptic fits.	The girl often has epileptic fits.	The girl very often has epileptic fits.

XXVIII. Aerophagia:

1.5		2.5		3.5	
1	2	3	4
The girl does not suffer from aerophagia or intestinal problems.	The girl sometimes suffers from aerophagia or intestinal problems.	The girl often suffers from aerophagia or intestinal problems.	The girl very often suffers from aerophagia or intestinal problems.

XXIX. Muscular tension:

1.5		2.5		3.5	
1	2	3	4
The girl has no muscular tension.	The girl has some muscular tension.	The girl has quite high muscular tension.	The girl has very high muscular tension.

XXX. Feeding habits:

1.5		2.5		3.5	
1	2	3	4
The girl always eats willingly.	The girl does not always eat willingly.	The girl often does not want to eat.	The girl never wants to eat.

XXXI. Overall impression:

1	1.5	2	2.5	3	3.5	4
The girl has no symptoms characteristic of Rett syndrome.		The girl has some symptoms characteristic of Rett syndrome.		The girl has many symptoms characteristic of Rett syndrome.		The girl has all the symptoms characteristic of Rett syndrome.

Appendix 5A.2

University of Messina
Department of Clinical and Experimental Medicine
Via Bivona, Messina
Mail: rafabio@unime.it

Prof. Rosa Angela Fabio

Anna Rossi's Diagnosis

Anna Rossi is born in Messina on xx/xx/xx. She shows Rett Syndrome with mutation c.808C>T (p. R270X) of MECP2 gene (NM-004992.3) (see Figure 5A.1).

Learning Area

The cognitive level is influenced by thoughts of dispersion of sustained selective attention. The development stage is similar to the sensorimotor stage. The subareas of the RARS, the cognitive, sensory, basic area, of the autonomies and of the typical characteristics, are presented in detail in Figure 5A.2 attached here.

Emotional-Affective Area

The girl presents both spontaneous and on demand eye-gaze, good partial indices of shared attention. In the social relationship she is very sensitive when she speaks with a low tone of voice, when she listens to the opera and when her parents cuddle her. He is able to communicate with the other, when he agrees and when he disagrees.

Linguisti Area

Anna has the ability to understand not only short sentences, but also interrelated sequences of two sentences. With reference to verbal production, the child is able to imitate the movement of the mouth thanks to the physical prompt, she is able to emit a sound similar to "a".

Sensory Area

Auditory, visual and functionality are normal. The child has hypersensitivity on auditory and even visual level. Anna presents very high levels of arousal that influences these aspects.

Area Motoria

Anna walks thanks to a support. As regards fine motor skills, and in particular the use of hands, the child touches objects but does so thanks to the help, which can be verbal or physical.

Neuropsychological Area

Anna presents hyper-activated levels of arousal; this activation determines a good capacity for understanding the elements of the exterior. His attention, however, is affected by the presence of stereotypy and self-stimulation. It tends to emit behaviors related to stereotypes such as: undulating and oscillatory movement of the head, rubbing of the hands, maintains if stimulated selective attention protracted over time, especially when effort is required.

Processi Mnestici

Anna remembers the places and environments

Orientamento Temporale

The child has not yet started the discrimination of temporal concepts.

Summary

Anna presents normally activated arousal levels and generalized attention. She has a good learning potential which is affected by the presence of head and hand stereotypes. With the suspension of these stereotypes, the attention improves. The potential learning is medium level. It is important to empowerment the ability to pay selective attention for a very long time, the ability to make specific discrimination and the ability to choose through the motor act.

Neuropsychological Assessment

Results of RARS

Cognitive area: 20
Sensory area: 3
Motor area: 8.5
Emotion area: 5
Autonomy area: 12
Features of RTT: 10
Behavioural features 12.5
Overall: 3.5

Results of Vineland

Communication: 28
Daily ability: 30
Socialitation: 46
Motor ability: 24

Goals of Cognitive Empowerment

Cognitive Area
1. Increase selective attention
2. Basic spatial discrimination - high/low
3. Large/small discrimination
4. Discrimination of quantities (tanti-pochi)
5. Discrimination of images 10 people and 10 objects
6. Discrimination of emotions

Linguistic Area
Vocal or letter production (ex. A, P ...)

Figure 5A.1 Degrees of severity of RTT identified = 41 = mild level.

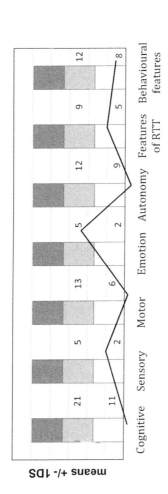

Figure 5A.2 Score in each area of RARS.

Motor Area
1. Refine the purposeful use of the hands
2. Maintenance and increase of functional units already acquired:
   a. Doing "hi" with your hand "
   b. Turn your head voluntarily and not as a stereotype
   c. Send kisses
   d. Increase the approach behavior of the hand towards objects by gradually moving the motivating stimuli presented to it.

Autonomy
1. Food education program
2. Program of autonomous movement in space

Communication
1. Activate and continue sound production
2. Language stimulation
3. Development of receptive language skills
4. Interventions to improve eye contact and direction
5. Developing visual and auditory attention to stimuli
6. Development of cognition and thinking skills

PROF. Rosa Angela Fabio

Chapter 6

Practical ways to manage the condition at school

In Italy, people with multiple disabilities, such as children with RTT, may go to state schools and can be educated alongside their non-disabled peers to the greatest extent possible. For children with RTT that need help, classroom teachers make changes in the classroom to meet the students' needs, such as modifications in the youngster's curriculum, the manner in which subjects are taught, homework assignments, and overall expectations. Throughout this process, it is essential that the child's strengths, including extracurricular activities, are nurtured and maintained. In this chapter, a practical way to manage the condition at school will be presented and a curriculum to teach children with RTT to read and learn will be proposed.

6.1 Cognitive empowerment methodologies

In Italy, the legislation dating back to the 1970s abolished special schools and nursery schools for children with disabilities. Inclusion in mainstream schools has been in effect since 1971. Special classes were abolished by law in 1977. However, in others countries of the world, the special schools for children with RTT are present, for example, in England, Ireland, Israel, the Czech Republic, and Unired States. In Italy, the children with RTT, or disability, take part in school activities in their classrooms together with other typically developing children. This is important because the girls with RTT have the possibility to interact with typically developing subjects in the school. Indeed, in several Italian studies, it was found that the interaction with others was a significant factor to improve the communication and social abilities in RTT (Antonietti, Castelli, Fabio, & Marchetti, 2002; Antonietti, Castelli, Fabio, & Marchetti, 2008; Castelli, Antonietti, Fabio, Lucchini, & Marchetti, 2013; Fabio, Giannatiempo, Oliva,

& Murdaca, 2011; Fabio, Castelli, Marchetti, & Antonietti, 2013; Fabio, Magaudda, Caprì, Towey, & Martino, 2018).

Moreover, in Italy, children with RTT have a personal teacher in the classroom. This teacher has a specific formation in education and disabilities.

In this chapter, an example of intervention and training with girls with RTT will be presented. Specifically, this intervention presents all the principles of cognitive empowerment which were discussed previously and concerns teaching girls with RTT to read and to write, in other words; learning to communicate.

6.1.1 Reading

The intervention arose from an initial reflection: if the clinician teaches RTT girls to communicate through artificial symbols that adults generally do not know – as they are those abstract symbols which are usually used with mentally retarded people – it would be very hard for these girls to communicate with other adults that do not know that artificial language. In other words, the possibilities for these girls to communicate would remain restricted to very few persons, the ones who share that artificial language. What the clinicians evinced by working with RS girls in the cognitive training previously described, is that they develop a very good knowledge of images, so we wondered: why do not try to teach them more abstract symbols, such as our common letters, starting from images in order to allow them to communicate through writing? The training about reading-writing abilities was made up of two phases (see Table 6.1).

Table 6.1 Phases of the intervention

FIRST PHASE

1. Evaluation of pre-requisites;
2. Discrimination of images of familiar objects and people.

SECOND PHASE

1. Discrimination of the image/word associations;
2. Bi/univocal correspondence between word and image (direct correspondence) and between image and word (indirect correspondence);
3. Separation of words into syllables and reconstruction;
4. Separation of syllables into letters and reconstruction;
5. Construction of sentences;
6. Communication.

6.2 The first phase of the intervention with RTT

Evaluation of pre-requisites, the girl started the reading-writing ability training once "equipped" with the basic concepts she had learnt in the previous training. Moreover, she had learnt a way of communication: she got accustomed to the presentation of two stimuli, to the request of looking at them and to choose the requested one either by looking at it and touching it (see Figure 6.1).

As far as the pre-requisites of the reading-writing ability training are concerned, the most relevant one is the girl's ability of reading images. Therefore a set of about 20 images are chosen: they were photos of important persons (parents, siblings, teachers ...) and of relevant objects (food, animals, toys) in the dimension of an A4 paper sheet (see Figures 6.2 & 6.3).

Discrimination of photos and images of familiar persons and objects.

To teach the girl to discriminate, initially the girl was presented one photo (target) with a distracter stimulus without any image (see Figure 6.4).

She was asked to look at them and to choose the target. Stimuli were presented in the randomized right-left order and only when the girl had reached the criteria for each image (she intentionally chose the target, so that the possibility of casual choices could be excluded) the other photos could be introduced with the same procedure. Once this step was reached for all 20 photos, they were reduced to the

Figure 6.1 An example of working with a girl with RTT.

Mother   Grand father   Sister

Figure 6.2 Examples of stimuli for discrimination of persons.

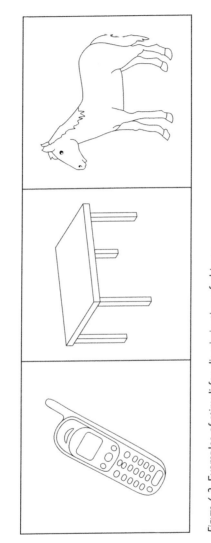

Figure 6.3 Examples of stimuli for discrimination of objects.

Figure 6.4 Example of discrimination of grandfather.

dimensions of 5×5, following the same methods and criteria. Finally, photos were substituted by drawings.

For instance the photo of the girl's horse was substituted with the drawing of a horse and gradually other images could be introduced, provided that they were part of the girl's world (a chair, a bed, a phone; see Figure 6.5). The discrimination procedure was the same as for photos.

6.3 The second phase of the intervention

6.3.1 Discrimination of the association image-word

The association image-word means that we present the child with one image and ask them choose between two words for a total of three times. We can move to the second phase if a child is able to choose the correct target. So if she or he doesn't work, we again present the image.

The work with words began in this phase. Twenty bi-syllable words were chosen: they must be words that interest the girl (such as "dad") and that are different in the letters (it is better to avoid words that start with "c" and "g" or with "p" and "b" as they are phonetically similar and hard to be discriminated). Each word was written on a white sheet, reporting also, in the first letter, the corresponding image and was presented with a distracter stimulus (a white sheet): the girl was asked to choose the stimulus with the affective word "dad" (see Figure 6.6). The procedure and the criteria were always the same.

The presentation of the correct stimulus was carried out with increasing difficulty of the distracter stimulus as in Figure 6.7.

6.3.2 Bi-univocal correspondence between word and image and between image and word

This work provided another proof of the intentionality of the girl's choices, as it allowed to exclude casual choices. In the direct correspondence the girl was presented one word, for instance "dad", and near it the images of dad and of another object (see Figure 6.8).

The girl was asked to choose the right image that corresponded to the word. In the indirect correspondence the girl was presented one image, for instance "dad", and near it the words of dad and of other objects (for instance: the word "dad" and another word; see Figure 6.9). The girl was asked to choose the right word that corresponded to the image.

Since the girl's fine motor skills were good, she was also asked to take the right image and put it on the word and vice versa; otherwise the girl can be helped by the educator. Separation of words into syllables and

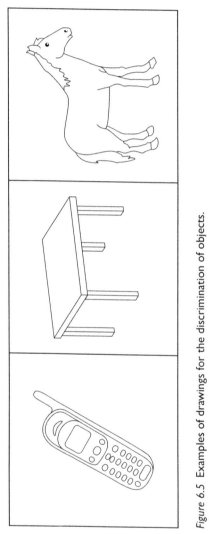

Figure 6.5 Examples of drawings for the discrimination of objects.

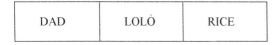

| DAD | LOLÒ | RICE |

Figure 6.6 Examples of stimuli for discrimination of words, "lolò" refers to the name of the sister of one of the girls.

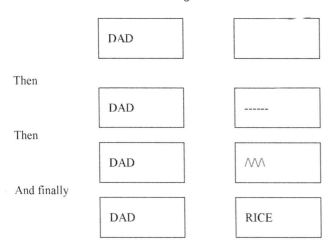

Figure 6.7 Example of the methodology for the discrimination of the word "dad".

reconstruction. The words that the girl had learnt were cut into syllables. The verb "cut" is used here literally: the girl watched the educator cutting words with scissors. For instance "mommy" was cut into "mo" and "mmy": the girl worked with syllables (see Figure 6.10).

She was asked to look at two syllables (the target syllable "mo" and a distracter syllable) and to choose the target one. In this way the girl learnt the first syllable, then the second, then the two target syllables were presented together and so on for every syllable of each word. After this step, the girl was asked to reconstruct the word: she was given the first syllable ("mo") and she was asked to choose the following syllable that completed the word "mommy" choosing it between two syllables or even among three ones. Finally, the girl had to do this work without the initial help of the first syllable: she was given some syllables and she was asked to build the word "mommy". In the last step, the girl was asked to build also new words that she had not learnt in the training but that were made up of the syllables she had learnt.

DAD

Figure 6.8 Example of correspondence.

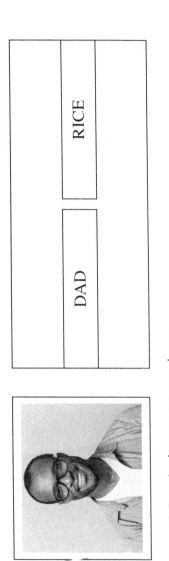

DAD	RICE

Figure 6.9 Example of inverse correspondence.

Figure 6.10 Example of work with the syllables.

Separation of syllables into letters and reconstruction. The same work with words and syllables was reproduced with letters: syllables were cut into single letters.

The previously described procedure was followed also with letters and at the end the girl was asked to build new words using letters.

1   Construction of sentences. The girl learnt to build short sentences using only two words. For instance, she was asked to build the sentence "dad eats" choosing the right letters from a group of many ones. At the beginning the girl needed plenty of time, since she had to choose among all the letters put in front of her; then she gradually became faster as the position of letters did not change; moreover, sentences gradually became longer.

2   The quality jump: communication. Initially, the girl was asked simple questions, such as "What is your name?", "Is mum here with you?", "What is mum's name?" and she was encouraged to answer using letters. In this case, the quality jump occurred: letters were not used to *reproduce* what the educator said anymore, but they were used for the *production* of an autonomous answer. Finally, the single letters were stuck on a big sheet of paper that became the alphabetic table the girl used to communicate. It can be easily rolled up and transported anywhere.

Children who can reach this goal compose words using their forefinger, as if the table were a computer keyboard. It is important that neither the educator, nor the mother, touch the girl's hands and arms while she is writing, as he/she has to do it by herself.

6.4 Rules at the school for students with RTT

Educational professionals and parents must understand the importance of rules and routines for individuals with RTT and apply them in various settings and situations. Application of rules and routines in school and home helps children with RTT engage more successfully in activities and prevents

Table 6.2 Examples of rules for teachers

Basic principles	Examples
Unconditional acceptance	When the girl arrives in the classroom, you can tell her: "I'm happy to meet you".
Rules	You can explain the daily routine to her: "Now, we will study with eye-tracker, after that, you will eat your food with your classmates, an then we will study with pictures". Do not say "you are angry, so I won't let you play you with your friends."
Reinforcement	When she correctly performs a task,you can tell her "great" or "very good" or you can give her favorite food.
Containment	When she has a hand stereotype, you can tell her: "Please, stop! Look at the eye-tracker".
Shaping	You can tell her "good" or give her her favorite food, when she shows a behavior that is close to the desired one, for example: look at the screen of eye-tracker, afterward look at the target for some seconds, then look at the target for a longer time.
Fading	You can help the girl to look at the target shown on screen eye-tracker by first orienting her head at the monitor until she looks the target. Gradually, you can remove your help by not orienting the head.

problem behavior. Routines help create an efficient environment. When the children know routines, they can perform daily activities more quickly. Rules and routines can be used at home and at school (see Table 6.2).

We suggest the following steps, that can be used at home and at school, to develop rules and routines for a subject with RTT:

1. Determining the most important rules or routines, because they can benefit from structure. Hence, to observe the student's daily routines and activities and prioritize individual needs.
2. Developing rules or desired behavior for a setting. Rules and routines can be developed differently depending on situations or people. For example, teachers can establish different rules for their classes. Rules need to be concise and observable. In addition, they should be stated using literally accurate and positive words to prevent confusion and posted in a visual format.
3. Teaching the rules directly. Once rules are established, teach them to the student directly. Direct instruction gives a rationale for the rule and provides knowledge about how to use the information. To teach rules and routines, teachers may use modeling or social narrative strategies. The adult may also teach rules using

behavioral strategies, including prompting, fading, shaping, and direct instruction. (For these methologies, see Chapter 4).
4. Providing support based on the student's age, interests, and individual needs. Visual supports of rules or routines are often very useful in enhancing student understanding of activities or sequences.
5. Evaluate and generalize rules and routines. Monitoring the student's progress is an important part of instruction. In addition, the student should eventually be able to generalize the rules and routines to various settings.
6. Write rules only in the positive. The rule should describe a specific behavior you want the student to perform and one that can be observed and practiced. Use basic language and no more than five to six words in the rule. Make sure the rules are relevant to the classroom setting and enforceable by all classroom personnel.

The following are others tips and guidelines on teaching rules to RTT girls:

1. Make sure you have the girl's attention before you deliver an instruction or ask a question;
2. Consider the girl's processing challenges and timing (for example, begin an instruction with the girl's name – this increases the likelihood that he may be attending by the time you deliver the direction);
3. Avoid complex verbal directions, information, and discussion. Keep instructions short or give information in chunks;
4. Give positive directions to allow for incomplete language processing;
5. Minimize the use of "don't" and "stop".
   This lets the girl know exactly what you want him to do;
6. Allow "wait time" (be prepared to wait for a response, whether it is an action or answer). Avoid immediately repeating an instruction or inquiry. Sometimes it is helpful to think of a student with auditory processing challenges like a computer – when it is processing, hitting the command again does not make it go any faster, but rather sends it back to the beginning to start the process all over again!
7. Model and shape correct responses to build understanding (for example, for a younger child, to teach the meaning of "stop": run on the playground holding hands with the student, say "stop"; stop yourself and the student; repeat until you can fade the hand-holding and then fade the modeling);

8. Supplement verbal information with pictures, visual schedules, gestures, visual examples, written directions.

However, it is important to point that children with RTT have limited skills in communication and other adaptive functioning, thus, rules and routines must be directly taught and thought for them. For example, as seen in Chapter 4, an activity schedule consisting of a set of pictures provides visual cues and helps the girl know the sequence of activities. Also, social stories are useful to introduce rules and routines.

6.5 Conclusion

In this chapter, we have described training to develop reading and writing abilities in RTT. Behavioral training based on the operant conditioning principles, as well as intervention in the communication, have been implemented with RTT patients. Other interventions have been focused on the use of special programmes and devices, including non-verbal training aimed at teaching basic and complex emotion recognition (in order to understand other people's behavior on the basis of mental states reasoning. In conclusion, we have supported the idea that if properly trained, the girls with RTT can reach higher developmental levels than those widely accepted in the literature thus far. Hence, we suggest the importance to include these subjects in the schools together with other typically developing people.

References

Antonietti, A., Castelli, I., Fabio, R.A., & Marchetti, A. (2002). Mental states comprehension in Rett syndrome, in IV European Conference: Psychological Theory and Research on Mental.

Antonietti, A., Castelli, I., Fabio, R.A., & Marchetti, A. (2008). Understanding emotions and mental states from faces and pictures in Rett Syndrome, in *Emotional Face Comprehension: Neuropsychological Perspectives* ed Balconi M., New York: Nova Science Publishers, 205–232.

Castelli, I., Antonietti, A., Fabio, R.A., Lucchini, B., & Marchetti, A. (2013). Do Rett syndrome persons possess Theory of Mind? Some evidence from non-treated girls. *Life Span and Disability*, 16, 2, 157–168.

Demeter, K. (2000). Assessing the developmental level in Rett syndrome: An alternative approach? *European Child Adolescent Psychiatry*, 9, 227–233. 10.1007/s007870070047.

Fabio, R.A., Magaudda, C., Caprì, T., Towey, G., & Martino, G. (2018). Choice Behavior in Rett syndrome, the consistency parameter. *Life Span and Disability*, 31, 1, 47–62.

Fabio R.A, Castelli I., Marchetti, A., & Antonietti, A. (2013). Training communication abilities in Rett syndrome through reading and writing. *Frontiers in Psychology*, *911*, 1–9.

Fabio, R.A., Giannatiempo, S., Oliva, P., & Murdaca, A.M. (2011). The increase of attention in Rett Syndrome. A pretest-post test research design. *Journal of Developmental and Physical Disability*, *23*, 99–111.

Hetzroni, O., Rubin, C., & Konkol, O. (2002). The use of assistive technology for symbol identification by children with Rett syndrome. *Journal Intellectual Development Disability*, *27*, 57–71. 10.1080/13668250120119626-1.

Lovaas, O.I., & Leaf, R. (1981). *Five Video Tapes for Teaching Developmentally Disabled Children*. Baltimore, MD: University Park Press.

Lotan, M., Isakov, E., & Merrick, J. (2004). Improving functional skills and physical fitness in children with Rett syndrome. *Journal Intellectual Development Disability*, *48*, 730–735. 10.1111/j.1365-2788.2003.00589.x.

Sigafoos, J., Laurie, S., & Pennell, D. (1995). Preliminary assessment of choice making among children with Rett syndrome. *JAPSH*, *20*, 175–184.

Smith, T., Klevstrand, M., & Lovaas, O.I. (1995). Behavioral treatment of Rett's disorder: Ineffectiveness in three cases. *Amercan Journal Mental Retardation*, *100*, 317–322.

Watson, J.S., Umansky, R., Marcy, S., & Repacholi, B. (1996). Intention and preference in a 3-year-old girl with Rett syndrome. *Journal of Applied Developmental Psychology*, *17*, 69–84. 10.1016/S0193-3973(96)90006-4.

Chapter 7

Rett Syndrome around the world

The aim of the present chapter is to study the conditions and features of individuals with Rett Syndrome (RTT) in different countries. To date, there is variability in knowledge and expertise between countries and variability in clinical practices both between and within countries. To our knowledge, no study has investigated the conditions of people with RTT associated with specific demographic characteristics. In the first part of this chapter, we will present an overview of the conditions related to RTT in countries within the European Union (EU), Australia, United States (US), and Eastern countries. In the second part, we will discuss some treatment differences between these countries. We will argue that some treatments, such as the inclusion in public school of individuals with RTT and access to cognitive empowerment from early childhood, can improve the quality of life.

7.1 EU conditions

The European Rett Syndrome Database Network (EuroRett) is a European initiative to promote research on rare diseases. It is a network of partners wanting to promote transnational network research on rare diseases. This program has been funded by the European Commission since 2006. The first call was launched in Spring 2007. In this context, several laboratories decided to join their forces to propose a European network on Rett Syndrome. We called our network EuroRETT and it was funded in 2007. Thanks to the EuroRETT network (see the next paragraph), a European Rett Syndrome database network was created. The database is now supervised by Prof. Alessandra Renieri in Siena (Italy). An executive committee was formed to review the proposals requesting the use of collected information. The executive committee is composed of clinicians who collected information on more than 50 patients. The EuroRett combines data from multiple sources and is more akin to the model of InterRett, but to date it has mainly been applied to investigations on epilepsy. The EuroRett has a different but valuable function, which is to catalog the variety of different genetic variants, both pathogenic and non-pathogenic, reported both in publications and from laboratories. This Database Network contains more than 2,000 patients over 13 different countries, collecting hundreds of items such as weight, size, age, and mutation for each individual. The prevalence of RTT in Europe has been estimated to be approximately 1/15,500.

A large amount of work has been performed by EuroRETT laboratories to understand neuronal dysfunction caused by MeCP2, CDKL5, or FOXG1 dysfunction. Alteration of the stability of microtubules and of neuronal trafficking was found, together with deficits of chromatin architecture, neuronal excitability, and morphology, or abnormal micro-RNA regulations in MeCP2deficient cells or tissues. Two EuroRETT laboratories performed in-depth studies of CDKL5 function, while others developed new mouse models.

In France, genetic laboratories are organized into a clinical and molecular network to investigate the incidence of RTT in the country. This network is supported by the Groupement d'Intérêt Scientifique (GIS)-Institut des maladies rares and the Association Française du Syndrome de Rett (a parent support group). The eight laboratories involved in this network (Paris Cochin, Paris Necker, Kremlin-Bicêtre, Nancy, Lyon, Rennes, Tours, Marseille) are geographically well distributed.

As of 2015, between five and ten European countries have either a national Rett expertise center or specialized multidisciplinary Rett clinics, some of which are embedded within centers for rare diseases. Several countries have one or more hospitals providing a diagnostic service and/or one or more medical experts offering advice and clinical management of the syndrome, whilst other European countries have no experts in RTT and rely on services aimed at general disabilities (Townend et al., 2016). In these cases, the role of the national parent association, where one exists, is especially crucial in supporting families and professionals.

7.2 Australia

As with European countries, Australia has also produced a population database on RTT. The Australian Rett Syndrome Database (ARSD) is a unique population-based registry of cases born since January 1976 to 2004. It has registered 276 verified female cases and 2 male cases. This database has already been used as a source of cases for a number of epidemiological, clinical, and radiological studies. Inclusion of molecular genetic data now enhances the registry and enables differentiation of those females with an identified MeCP2 mutation. Some studies using the ARSD have indicated the increasing availability of MeCP2 genetic diagnostic testing, as well as a greater knowledge of the disorder among clinicians, and a change of the pattern and timing of diagnosis. More precisely, the prevalence of RTT among 5- to 18-year-olds was significantly higher in 2004 than that found in the 1997 study. Laurvick and colleagues (2006) argued that the increase could be attributed to the availability of molecular testing, as well as earlier and improved diagnoses because pediatricians and child neurologists have a better awareness of the disorder and its clinical variability. Moreover, the authors claimed that the advances in technology (e.g. the growing use of percutaneous gastrostomy feeding) improved outcomes and led to less mortality within this population. In conclusion, the epidemiology of RTT in Australia has changed and genetic testing has made it possible for cases to be diagnosed at a younger age before a full "Rett phenotype" has developed.

7.3 Eastern countries

To date, in Japan, 218 different mutations have been reported in a total of more than 2,100 patients. In the study by Fukuda and colleagues (2005), 45 different mutations of MeCP2 were identified in 145 of 219 (66.2%) female patients with classical or atypical RTT, 74 patients (33.6%), including 16 with classical RTT who did not have a MeCP2 mutation in the entire coding and flanking regions. Also, in this study, MeCP2 mutations were found in 115 of 131 patients with classical RTT (87.8%), but in 30 of 88 patients with atypical RTT (34.1%).

On the contrary, the molecular characteristics of RTT in China are unknown. Only one study delineated the molecular characteristics of RTT in China based on the largest group of Chinese patients ever studied (Zhang et al., 2012), for which 365 Chinese patients with Rett syndrome were recruited. MeCP2, CDKL5, and FOXG1 mutational analysis were performed. Moreover, the parental origin of mutated MeCP2 gene, the MeCP2 gene mutation rate in the patients' mothers, and the X-chromosome inactivation pattern of the mothers who carry the mutation were analyzed. The results of this study were varied: 315 had MeCP2 gene mutations and 3 had de novo CDKL5 gene mutations. No patients had the FOXG1 mutation. Among the 315 cases with MeCP2 mutations, 264 were typical cases and 41 were atypical cases. All the three cases with CDKL5 gene mutations were atypical RTT with early-onset seizures. MeCP2 gene mutations were found in 86.3% patients, and CDKL5 gene mutations were found in 21.4% patients with early-onset seizure variant. It is interesting to note that FOXG1 mutations were not found in this group of Chinese patients, whereas in other countries of the word, this mutation is present. With reference to parental mutations, it was found that 94.4% cases with mutations were from paternal origin and 5.6% were from maternal origin.

In conclusion, the work of Zhang and colleagues (2012) is the first systematic research of the molecular characteristics of Chinese population with RTT. Thus, future studies are needed to understand in deeper the features of people with RTT in China. This is important both for demographic and medical reasons.

7.4 Israel

The Israel Rett Syndrome Foundation (IRSF) is an Israeli non-profit organization. It was established in 2001 to coordinate all efforts and needs associated with RTT. It is the only organization of its kind addressing the wellbeing needs of this specific population in Israel. This foundation serves some 1,000 people a year from all over Israel, which includes the patients, their families, and professionals. Aside from its efforts to seek funding for medical research to find a cure, the IRSF seeks to raise funds to provide for the best possible quality of life for Israelis suffering from RTT and their families. The program offers support, relevant knowledge, training, and advocacy to improve the quality of life for sufferers. More precisely, the services of the proposed activities are as follows:

Families are provided with guidance, consultations, and support through:

1. Educational and social meetings with parents and other family members of Rett syndrome patients;
2. Dissemination of professional literature for families, caregivers, family support groups assisting families to access government benefits and entitlements;
3. Dissemination of knowledge and seminars and training for professionals in the medical and paramedical fields;

4. The foundation advocates on behalf of the victims and their families within the governmental, legislative, medical, educational, and social systems. The foundation belongs to a Rare Diseases coalition that meets with Israeli MPs and Ministry of Health officials in an effort to legislate a rare diseases law.

In 2003, the association called Israel Rett Syndrome Center (IRSC) was established and managed by families of girls with RTT. The main aim of the IRSC was to improve the quality of life for individuals with RTT and their families. This goal should be attained through several activities:

1. Promoting awareness of RS among the general public and among the medical and paraprofessional community, in view of the syndrome's rarity;
2. Providing support and counseling for parents of individuals with RTT;
3. Assessing individuals with RTT by means of a team of experts;
4. Providing guidance for educators and therapists working with individuals with RTT;
5. Promoting and funding research on RTT (Lotan et al., 2006).

To achieve these purposes, two structures were established: the Rett Syndrome Medical Clinic at the Safra Children's Hospital, Sheba Medical Center at Tel-Hashomer and the rehabilitation/education assessment and counseling group of the IRSC.

7.5 United States (US)

In the US, the estimate is that Rett syndrome affects between 1 in 10,000 and 1 in 22,000 females. The International Rett Syndrome Association (IRSA) North American database is the first comprehensive compilation of information in the US and Canada on individuals with RTT or with another diagnosis in association with MeCP2 mutations. The North American database is derived principally from members of IRSA, in which membership is voluntary. Therefore, this database is not population-based. However, the large number of participants should be generally representative of RTT within the US and Canada. The results contained in this database indicate that the distribution of MeCP2 mutations among the 914 participants with positive testing is similar to published data, in particular the larger series from France and Italy.

The International Rett Syndrome Foundation (IRSF) has created an innovative clinic program, designating 14 clinics in the US as RTT Clinical Research Centers of Excellence. At the heart of these Clinical Research Centers is a team of specialists with substantial experience in the diagnostic evaluation and treatment of individuals with RTT. Physician specialists, nurses, therapists, and care managers all support the individuals' care management and coordination. The 14 Centers of Excellence are the following:

1. Alabama – University of Alabama Birmingham Civitan International Research Center, Birmingham;
2. California – University of California San Diego, Rady Children's Hospital, San Diego;
3. California – University of California San Francisco, Benioff Children's Hospital Oakland, Walnut Creek;
4. Colorado – Children's Hospital Colorado, Aurora;
5. Illinois – Rush University Medical Center, Chicago;
6. Massachusetts – Boston Children's Hospital and Harvard Medical School;
7. Minnesota – Gillette Children's Specialty Healthcare, Saint Paul;
8. Missouri – Washington University School of Medicine, Saint Louis Children's Hospital, Saint Louis;
9. New York – University of Rochester Medical Center, Rochester;
10. Ohio – Cincinnati Children's Hospital Medical Center, Cincinnati;
11. Pennsylvania – Children's Hospital of Philadelphia, Philadelphia;
12. South Carolina – Greenwood Genetic Center, Greenwood;
13. Tennessee – Vanderbilt University School of Medicine and Vanderbilt Kennedy Center for Research on Human Development, Nashville;
14. Texas – Texas Children's Hospital, The Blue Bird Circle Rett Center, Houston.

7.6 Treatment differences between countries

The management of RTT is mainly symptomatic and individualized, focusing on aiming to optimize each patient's abilities. A dynamic multidisciplinary approach is most effective, with specialist input from dietitians, physiotherapists, occupational therapists, speech therapists, and music therapists. However, clinical management has improved considerably from the time when RTT was first recognized.

Individuals with RTT need multiple assistance and health care. Indeed, they generally use more health services than other people with disabilities. Health service use in RTT has been examined by some researchers. A pilot study focused on the burden and impact of RTT, and factors such as functional abilities, medical needs, and the use of medical therapy and accommodation services were explored. Participants consisted of 86 mainly US families. Significant differences were found in the use of medical services by age group, with visits to pediatricians, geneticists, and neurologists decreasing with age and visits to general practitioners increasing with age.

Moore and colleagues (2005) examined the use and pattern of health service utilization in RTT in Australia. Multivariate analysis indicated that genetic, clinical, and socio-demographic factors were all significant predictors of the utilization of medical services. Health status and health service use was examined considering age and mutation type. Results indicated that although the health status declined with age, health service use was also shown to decline in parallel. However, these patterns differed by mutation type, thus demonstrating important variability.

Hendrie and colleagues (2011) examined use and cost of health sector and related services in RTT and effects of socio-demographic, clinical severity, and genetic factors on costs. Participants were individuals with RTT registered with the ARTT Database in 2004. Their results indicated that people with RTT had a higher utilization of health services. Attendance with medical and dental practitioners was extremely high, as was the use of non-durable health-related products. Other resources used regularly by the majority of cases included therapy services out of school and paid home and community services, medical tests not involving an admission to hospital, prescription and non-prescription regular medications and supplements, prescriptions for acute conditions, and therapeutic devices and special equipment. Utilization patterns reported in this study were similar to those of a previous Australian study mentioned previously (Moore et al., 2005).

In Italy, the subjects with RTT live with their family. Legislation dating back to the 1970s abolished special schools and nursery schools for children with disabilities. Inclusion in mainstream schools has been in effect since 1971. Special classes were abolished by law in 1977. However, suitable services for people with RTT are sorely lacking.

In some countries of the world, special schools for children with RTT are present. For example, 12 special schools that are active in EnglandSpecial schools are also present in Ireland, whereas in the Czech Republic, the Rett girls' education is organized as a combination of group and individual lessons. The girls take part either in an activity in their classrooms together with other children with various, mainly combined disabilities, or they attend different school lessons and therapies, according to their individual study plans. Among the therapies are, for example: physiotherapy, ergo-therapy, canine therapy, music-therapy, basal stimulation, hippo-therapy, water-therapy, or swimming. The girls also visit a special therapy room – snooze-land, a musictherapy room, or visual room.

In Israel,

> The purpose of special education is to promote and develop the skills and abilities of exceptional children, and to correct and improve their physical, mental, emotional, and behavioral functioning. Its purpose is to give them knowledge, skills, and habits that teach them acceptable behavior in society, to facilitate their integration into normal life and work.

In accordance with this act, the Magshimim School for adults and children who have been diagnosed with various pervasive developmental disorders, such as autism, Asperger syndrome, Rett Syndrome, and others was established.

In the US, the Office of Overseas Schools (A/OPR/OS) is staffed with regional education officers, each assigned oversight of a geographic region, who are well-informed about schools attended by US government employees' school-age dependent children.

In conclusion, the biggest difference between countries in the conditions of treatment is the presence or absence of special schools for children with RTT. This is important because the girls with RTT have the opportunity to interact with typically developing subjects at the school in Italy. Moreover, in Italy for each group of symptoms of the RTT disease, there are specific treatments. In particular, for the Italian clinicians, the empowerment of cognitive, emotional, and communication skills are very important. It seems that in the other countries of the world, they are not given this same importance.

7.7 Parents' associations

As seen in this and Chapter 3, living with RTT is complex and the parents take care of their children with RTT for all their lives. Some parents are comforted by the knowledge that a number of organizations dedicate their resources to helping people with RTT. These

Table 7.1 Parent associations in the world

Country	Parents' association name and website
Austria	*Österreichische Rett-Syndrom Gesellschaft (ÖRSG)* www.rett-syndrom.at
Belgium	*Belgische Rett Syndroom Vereniging* www.rettsyndrome.be
Bulgaria	No Rett parent association registered with *RSE*
Croatia	No Rett parent association registered with *RSE*
Cyprus	No Rett parent association registered with *RSE* *Pancyprian Association for Rare Genetic Disorders "Unique Smiles"* offers support to families via Facebook
Czech Republic	*Rett Community Association* www.rett-cz.com/cz
Denmark	*Landsforeningen Rett Syndrom* www.rett.dk
Estonia	No Rett parent association registered with *RSE*
Finland	*Rett Finland (formerly Autistien ja Rett-henkiloiden Tuki ry, AURE ry)* www.aure.fi
France	*Association Francaise du Syndrome de Rett (AFSR)* Founded 1988 https://afsr.fr
Germany	*Elternhilfe fur Kinder mit Rett-Syndrom in Deutschland e.V.* www.rett.de
Greece	*Αγγελοι γης ("Angels on Earth")* www.rettgreece.gr
Hungary	*Magyar Rett Szindroma Alapitvany* www.rettszindroma.hu
Iceland	*Gudruns Rett Syndrome Research Trust* www.rettenglar.yolasite.com
Ireland	*The Rett Syndrome Association of Ireland* www.rettsyndrome.ie
Italy	*Associazione Italiana Rett (AIRETT)* www.airett.it *ProrRettricerca* www.prorett.org/
Latvia	No Rett parent association registered with *RSE*
Lithuania	No Rett parent association registered with *RSE* *Lietuvos autizmo asociacija "Lietaus vaikai"(Lithuania* *Autism Association)* offers support to families www.lietausvaikai.lt
Luxembourg	No Rett parent association registered with *RSE* *Autisme Luxembourg asbl* offers support to families *ALAN – Rare Diseases Luxembourg* also supports families www.alan.lu
Malta	No Rett parent association registered with *RSE*

(*Continued*)

Table 7.1 (Continued)

Country	Parents' association name and website
Netherlands	Nederlands Rett Syndroom Vereniging (NRSV) Founded 2008 www.rett.nl Stichting Terre – Dutch Rett Syndrome Foundation www.stichtingterre.nl
Norway	Norsk Forening for Rett Syndrom www.rettsyndrom.no
Poland	Ogolnopolskie Stowarzyszenie Pomocy Osobom Z Zespołem Retta (OSPOzZR) http://rettsyndrome.pl
Portugal	Associacao Nacional de Pais e Amigos Rett (ANPAR) http://anpar.planetaclix.pt
Romania	Asociatia "Un inger pentru ingeri" ("An angel for the angels") www.asociatiauningerpentruingeri.ro
Slovakia	Rett Slovakia (Nadacia pre pomoc ľud'om postihnutym Rettovym syndromom-Slovensko) No website
Slovenia	Tihi angeli ("Quiet angels") – not currently active
Spain	Asociacion Espanola de Sindrome de Rett www.rett.es Asociacion Catalana del Sindrome de Rett www.rettcatalana.es
Sweden	Rett syndrome I Sverige (RSIS) www.rsis.se
UK	Rett UK www.rettuk.org

associations can become invaluable sources of information and advice. Many associations offer parent support, financial assistance, and other important services. In this chapter, we illustrated the parent associations present in the different countries of the world. The goal is helping the families living with RTT in the research of information. See Table 7.1 showing the parents' associations present in the world.

7.8 Conclusion

In summary, RTT is found in all racial and ethnic groups throughout the world. It is important to recognize that the people affected by RTT may have difficulty communicating verbally and physically, that they experience a full range of emotions and understand more than they can express. They have engaging personalities and will enjoy taking part in social, educational, and recreational activities at home and in the community.

References

Christodoulou, J., Grimm, A., Maher, T. & Bennetts, B. (2003). RettBASE: the IRSA MECP2 variation database – a new mutation database in evolution. *Human Mutation*, *21*, 466–472.

Fukuda, T. et al. (2005). Methyl-CpG binding protein 2 gene (MECP2) variations in Japanese patients with Rett syndrome: pathological mutations and polymorphisms. *Brain & Development*, *27*, 211–217.

Hendrie, D., Bebbington, A., Bower, C. & Leonard, H. (2011). Measuring use and cost of health sector and related care in a population of girls and young women with Rett syndrome. *Research in Autism Spectrum Disorders*, *5*, 901–909.

Laurvick, C.L. et al. (2006). Rett syndrome in Australia: a review of the epidemiology. *The Journal of Pediatrics*, *148*(3), 347–352.

Moore, H., Leonard, H., Fyfe, S., de Klerk, N. & Leonard, N. (2005). InterRett – the application of bioinformatics to international Rett syndrome research. *Annals of Human Biology*, *32*, 228–236.

Townend, G.S., Smeets, E., van Waardenburg, D., van der Stel, R., van den Berg, M., van Kranen, H.J. & Curf, L. (2016). Rett syndrome and the role of national parent associations within a European context. *Rare Diseases and Orphan Drugs*, *2*(2), 17–26.

Zhang, Z. et al. (2012). Molecular characteristics of Chinese patients with Rett Syndrome. *European Journal of Medical Genetics*, *55*, 677–681.

Glossary

Adaptive Behaviors: Behaviors that increase reproductive success.

Alpha Waves: Type of brain waves present when a person is very relaxed or meditating.

Alternate-Forms Reliability: The ability of a test to produce the same results when two different versions of it are given to the same group of people.

Ambiguous Language: Language that can be understood in several ways.

Amplitude: The height of a wave.

Amygdala: A part of the limbic system of the brain that is involved in regulating aggression and emotions, particularly fear.

Assimilation: The broadening of an existing schema to include new information.

Anterior cingulate cortex (ACC): The anterior cingulate cortex (ACC) is the frontal part of the cingulate cortex.

Apraxia: A neurological syndrome characterized by loss of skilled or purposeful movement that cannot be attributed to weakness or an inability to innervate the muscles.

Baseline: Serves as a value with which to compare the values of the ongoing processes during an explicit task.

Beta Waves: The type of brain waves present when a person is awake and alert.

Brain: The main organ in the nervous system.

Brain Waves: Tracings that show the electrical activity of the brain.

Broca's Area: A part of the brain, in the left frontal lobe, that is involved in speech production.

Central Nervous System: The part of the nervous system that includes the brain and the spinal cord.

Cerebellum: The cerebellum is a region of the brain that has been ascribed an important role in motor control.

Cognition: Thinking. It involves mental activities such as understanding, problem-solving, decisionmaking, and creativity.

Conditioned Response: In classical and operant conditioning, a response that resembles an unconditioned response, achieved by pairing a conditioned stimulus with an unconditioned stimulus.

Conditioned Stimulus: In classical conditioning, a neutral stimulus that comes to evoke a response similar to an unconditioned response through pairing with an unconditioned stimulus.

Continuous Reinforcement: A reinforcement schedule in which reinforcement happens every time a particular response occurs.

Diagnosis: The process of distinguishing among disorders.

Diagnostic and Statistical Manual of Mental Disorders (DSM): A reference book used by psychologists and psychiatrists to diagnose psychological disorders.

Electroencephalograph (EEG): A device that records the overall electrical activity of the brain via electrodes placed on the scalp.

Encoding: The process of putting information into memory.

Event-related functional magnetic resonance imaging (efMRI): Event-related functional magnetic resonance imaging is a technique in magnetic resonance imaging that can be used to detect changes in the Blood Oxygen Level Dependent hemodynamic response to neural activity in response to certain events.

Event-related Potential (ERP): A change in electrical activity that is time-locked to specific events, such as the presentation of a stimulus or the onset of a response.

Family Studies: Studies in which researchers examine trait similarities among members of a family to figure out whether that trait might be inherited.

Family Therapy: A type of therapy in which a therapist sees two or more members of a family at the same time.

Frequency bands: Formations of neural oscillations that can be found in EEG, MEG, or local field potentials.

Hippocampus: A part of the limbic system involved in memory.

Hypothalamus: A part of the forebrain that helps to control the pituitary gland, the autonomic nervous system, body temperature, and biological drives.

Mean: The arithmetic average of a set of scores.

Motivation: An internal process that makes a person move toward a goal.

Motor Development: The increasing coordination of muscles that makes physical movements possible.

Neurons: Nervous system cells that communicate via electrochemical signals.

Neurotransmitters: Chemicals that are released from a neuron and activate another neuron.

P300:   An evoked potential which occurs as a response to stimuli which are unexpected, infrequent, or motivationally relevant.

Positive Reinforcement: In operant conditioning, the presentation of a stimulus after a response so that the response will be more likely to occur.

Primary Auditory Cortex: In the temporal lobe of the cerebrum, the brain part involved in processing auditory information.

Primary Motor Cortex: In the frontal lobe of the cerebrum, the brain part involved in controlling muscle movement.

Recall: The process of remembering without any external cues.

Recognition: The process of identifying learned information by using external cues.

Reinforcement: The delivery of a consequence that increases the likelihood that a response will occur.

Reinforcement Schedule: The pattern in which reinforcement is given over time.

Retrieval: The process of getting information out of memory.

Selective Attention: The ability to focus on some pieces of sensory information and ignore others.

Working Memory: An active memory system that holds information while it is processed or examined.

Index

Printed in Great Britain
by Amazon

18591031R00078